On The Night He Was Betrayed

(Treachery and Betrayal in the Church)

Pearl Coleman

New Wine Press

New Wine Press
PO Box 17
Chichester
West Sussex PO20 6YB
England

Unless otherwise stated all Bible quotations are from the
Authorised Version.

The Amplified Bible © Copyright 1965 Zondervan
Publishing House, Grand Rapids, Michigan MI 49506, USA.
KJV – King James Version.
NIV – The Holy Bible, New International Version. Copyright
© 1973, 1978, International Bible Society, published by
Hodder & Stoughton.

ISBN: 1 874367 34 5

Typeset by CRB Associates, Norwich
Printed in England by Clays Ltd, St Ives plc.

Contents

Dedication

This book is dedicated to Rev. Marion Daniel of Sozo Ministries International whose word of knowledge set me free from treachery, and triggered this extraordinary revelation which has set so many of the Church's wounded free.

Acknowledgement

Acknowledgment and my love and thanks go to my secretary Ruth Daniels who made it possible for me to produce this manuscript in such a short time following the revelation. May the Lord bless her and continue to heal her, in Jesus' name.

Foreword

The insights contained within the covers of this book could only have been given by the Holy Spirit.

Having been involved for many years in the ministry of deliverance, I have no doubt that this book has been inspired by the Holy Spirit. It is based soundly on the Word of God. As a result of reading the manuscript, I have already proven in my own experience the truths contained in it. I have no doubt that many thousands will be set free as the principles set out herein are applied widely in the Body of Christ.

I would commend this book to anybody involved in Christian counselling. It contains a simple but profound truth which will be the key to the healing and deliverance of a great number of people.

Bill Subritzky

Introduction

Pearl asked me to read this book largely because of my own recent involvement with its contents, and because I was subsequently led to go to the Clinic to be prayed for by the ministry team, at a time of great need. After a period of worship to begin that evening meeting, all sixteen of us waited quietly on God. I thought that the contributions people had to share afterwards were accurate and profound, without exception. No one except Pearl had any previous knowledge of what had been going on in my life. I found this most encouraging.

I believe this book holds out a lifeline for people like myself, who feel they have been the victims of treachery, but wonder deep down if they have not brought it all on themselves by their own folly. But please be warned. This book may not be easy material for you to handle.

I think of this book as a mine. This idea is biblical; the search for wisdom is compared to digging for precious stones in Job 28. The analogy is worth pursuing. Our phrase 'a mine of information' has come to suggest someone who is an easy source of ideas, but real mining is harder work. Much useless earth has to be shifted, at great effort and cost. The word 'boring', which has passed into our culture, says it all. Mining requires dedication. True prospectors do not give up digging simply because they hit hard rock.

This book contains ground that I suspect many will find hard. Some passages seem inaccessible to the point of being granite-like, to my mind, although personally I never found the book boring. Several times during it we are given drill to do, and maybe you will be tempted not to practise this material and pass on, like me. I suspect this will be to our loss; there is no short cut to doing the drilling if you wish to find gold.

To the patient and the committed there are gems to be found here, even if some are covered with earth and hard to recognise at first glance. I recommend that you ponder this book. I appreciated the passage about the abcess in particular. Also, I never understood what 'lifting the heel' meant before.

I suspect that some readers will be on the verge of despair over personal relationships. This book gives us practical help to persevere. Recently I remembered Jacob's dream of the ladder to heaven and the blessing of God on his life (Genesis 28). Then I flicked back a few pages to see what he had done previously and found treachery of the first order; Jacob impersonating his brother, deceiving his father, the cause of a rift between his parents, and provoking Esau to murder (Genesis 27). And yet, far from giving up on him, God still loved him! I could hardly fathom it. This story motivates me not to give up on my brother, even if he kicks me in the teeth, as Jacob had done to his family, and to God.

I find Jonah also a source of great encouragement. After behaving wickedly, Jonah was flung overboard by his companions and sank without trace. Surely this was the end. Yet it turned out to be the prelude to him becoming the most effective evangelist the world has yet seen, to my mind. And here's the good part – it happened even though his attitude was still far from right. His near death led to repentance that was only partial. God has everything under control, and even human wickedness is clay in His hands, with potential for good. There is hope for us all.

The danger with a book on treachery may be that it encourages me to see myself as the victim, and so to fix the blame on others, but Pearl clearly shows in this book what is almost like a cross-infection of treachery. Praise God that when I finally see some of my own faults, and begin to grasp how badly I have behaved, I am not to lose hope because God still loves me (Romans 5:8). Neither am I to hate myself. No way will I be rejected, even if I find it almost impossible in practice to learn better ways of loving others (John 6:37).

I commend this book to you. May you benefit from this wisdom of Pearl's.

Rev. Dr David F. Pennant

13

Prologue

You may wonder what on earth my photograph with such a handsome gentleman is doing on the front of this book. This very special man is Jason, my husband, through whom I learned about the ramifications of Hinduism, Asian strongholds like the Chinese Dragon, and martial arts. The photograph was taken on 3rd October 1993 following my ministry to him to break many of those strongholds, from which I praise God he was set free. Without knowing Jason I doubt if this book would have ever been written.

I wish to announce to readers that Jason and I married in Malaysia on 7th January 1993 in an Islamic Civil Office, and yes, he is the same man accompanying me with his guitar pictured on the cover of *Fruit Abiding in the Vine* some five years ago. If you compare the two photographs you can see the wonderful effects of deliverance, all praise be to the Lord Jesus!

Our very painful testimony, which ultimately has been for the glory of God, is told in my next book *Refined by Fire*. Jason is a former heroin addict whose amazing testimony of the Lord's mercy and healing will be given in this book. It illustrates God's mercy and the need for endurance, as it is written in Matthew 24:13,

> *'He that shall endure unto the end, the same shall be saved.'*

Our Christian Wedding/Blessing took place in England on 16th October 1994, with 135 dear brothers and sisters in Christ and a few unsaved. Our Pastor, the Rev. Marion Daniel, conducted a holy ceremony from Ephesians. The ceremony had a rich African dimension provided by the anointed praise and worship of the choir and musicians of Forward in Faith Ministries, Edgware, my lovely African bridesmaids Nyakwera Bazarrabusa and Margaret Appiagyei, and Rufus Adu, my long time right-hand man in ministry, as Master of Ceremonies.

Dr Hamish Rae, also with me many years, Lesley Whitehead and my assistant Henrietta Hillier were our Ushers. Henrietta's husband Warren, also a very supportive team member, was Jason's best man. The soloist dancer Jacqui Rendall and guitar soloist Vivienne Oates delighted us all with very special music and dancing unto the Lord.

First preference was given to the Jews, of which ancestry I believe I am. The anointing on the whole assembly has been much commented upon and healings, a miracle, and much repentance and repair of stale marriages took place. The wonderful news is still arriving! The day was one of great joy and proof that God completes what He has begun, praise His name!

16

Chapter 1

End Time Message for the Church

I have just completed my fourth book *Jehovah Jireh* and I had no idea that I should be following hard on the heels of this publication with another book, and yet the Holy Spirit has called me in no uncertain manner to write it.

It is with great awe and in the fear of the Lord that I set down what I believe to be an end time message for the Church. But first, it is vital to define what I mean by the Church. I take it to mean what is described in Matthew 18:20:

> *'For where two or three are gathered together in My name, there am I in the midst of them.'*

Why on earth God should choose somebody like me to bring such a message to His Church I have no idea, but then I always trust His intentions. He will know how this will or can be done. He will open and shut doors for me, I can depend on that!

In ministry and teaching the Body of late I have

constantly emphasised that God is looking for no-bodies like me, that he is fed up with named ministries who have a great razzmatazz that sur-rounds them; that He is finding the noise of some music groups we are deafened by in Churches an abominable din, and much else.

I do realise of course that many of these Church music groups believe that worldly music can draw people from the world into the Church by identifica-tion. That may indeed be true in the first instance, but I dare to say that this noise, for one can only call it that, may lure them into the Church, but it will cer-tainly not keep them there! Such newcomers will ulti-mately be searching for something different to the world they want to escape from. Do not let the Devil deceive you on that!

In an assembly abroad recently I had to tear up tissues and put them in my ears because I found the music so deafening. In fact had the Lord not been requiring me to stand in that assembly in a particular position, I would have certainly left smartly. The shock too of the choir actually clicking their fingers like disco singers as they sang was another horror.

I am not judging, I am not condemning, I am stat-ing a fact. I believe that the Lord wants to be wor-shipped in the beauty of holiness, in Spirit and in truth. The Holy Spirit is such a gentleman, so quiet and gentle, that I do not feel that He can come in such a din.

There are many other tough things I have been say-ing to the Body of Christ recently. However, I always emphasise that every word is spoken in love. Love sometimes has to be tough. I do not believe that we have a wishy-washy Jesus, but somebody who calls things what they are.

I believe with countless other Christians that we are living in end times. I want to stress that this does not stop me living and working in the here and now, rather the reverse. Whatever the time, whether it is near or far, I would be a slave to His will and directions. He is my first love.

Ever since 1994 began, a passage from the Holy Bible has been constantly quickened in my spirit. It is 2 Timothy 3:1–5:

> 'This know also, that in the last days perilous times shall come. For men shall be lovers of their own selves, covetous, boasters, proud, blasphemers, disobedient to parents, unthankful, unholy, Without natural affection, trucebreakers, false accusers, incontinent, fierce, despisers of those that are good, Traitors, heady, highminded, lovers of pleasures more than lovers of God: Having a form of godliness, but denying the power thereof: from such turn away.'

In those verses four things have been specifically and constantly highlighted. They are; the perilous times, false accusers, traitors and having a form of godliness.

There is so much out there which has a form of godliness, I am sure readers would agree. We need therefore to pray daily the prayer for revelation against deception, which I have mentioned and had printed in three of my books already. I make no excuse for repeating it yet again, for it has been my lifeline often, and I know from the correspondence I have received concerning this prayer that it has availed much.

As I have also said before, be prepared for shocks when you pray it from your heart but, believe me, the greatest gift we are needing during these perilous times is the gift of the discerning of spirits and of one particular spirit under Jezebel: deception, which includes alas self-deception. Deception is everywhere, folks. Beware!

Prayer for Revelation Against Deception

Father, in the name of Jesus, please send your Holy Spirit of truth to guide me into all truth and show me things to come (John 16:13). Please give me revelation knowledge and unveil all deception around me, remove scales from my eyes and unstop my deaf ears so that I may hear and see what the Spirit of the Lord would have revealed to me.

Thank You, Father, that when I call unto You, You show me great and mighty things which I know not (Jeremiah 33:3). I am calling unto You now according to your Word, that You set an end to darkness, and bring all that is hidden to light (Job 28:3 & 11). Thank You that according to Your Word there is nothing covered that shall not be revealed and hidden that shall not be known (Matthew 10:26).

Praise be to Your name, that it is written that You will give me the treasures of darkness and hidden riches of secret places (Isaiah 45:3), that You reveal the deep and secret things and know what is in the darkness and the light dwells in

You (Daniel 2:22), for You are the God of heaven who reveals secrets (Daniel 2:28).

Thank you, precious Holy Spirit, for guiding me into all truth this day and always. Praise be to the name of our God for ever and ever. Let every hidden thing be revealed according to His Word, Amen.

(*Note:* 'Me' and 'I' can be substituted with 'us' and 'we'.)

Chapter 2

The Curse of Treachery and Betrayal

Having got that off my chest, please, dear readers, know that everything that follows is brought to you in the deep, deep love of Jesus. When I ministered this word recently to congregations and smaller assemblies and groups in Penang I emphasised at the onset of every gathering that

> 'This is a hard message, but it is brought to you in love.'

The excitement and delight I experienced when I saw people in assemblies being so set free and released by this teaching as a result of their receiving it in love is beyond description. My heart was filled with such joy and peace and gratitude to the Holy Spirit for His revelations.

What I am about to share with readers now could have the same lifechanging effect it has had already on so many others, including my own precious fellowship Sozo Ministries International, and many of my patients who unwittingly highlighted for me, as I ministered to them at various times passing through the Clinic as physical patients in the first instance, the prolific evidence of the curse of treachery and betrayal in the Body of Christ.

How did it all begin? Well, I would refer readers to my third book *The Anointing Breaks the Yoke*. You may recall in Chapter 27 entitled 'Thank You, Jesus' my incredible healing from ME after a long struggle against its debility.

I ended up at Sozo Ministries where Marion Daniel, a beautiful ordained minister of God who is now my Pastor, received a word for me that set me free in Jesus' holy name. She received the word **'treachery'**, and also that I had been sent an angel of light whose activities she decommissioned.

My dead limbs literally sprang into life, my depression fled and I was instantly totally restored to my former vibrant self. Every part of me was energised by the Holy Spirit as I was cut free. I remember it so well. It was not a gradual recovery but an instantaneous, complete healing.

How extraordinary is our God who will give such a revelation by His Spirit, and ultimately cause the bringer of the revelation to receive its benefits for themselves! It's like the casting of one's bread on the waters, so that it returns in so many days.

> *'Cast thy bread upon the waters; for thou shalt find it after many days.'*   (Ecclesiastes 11:1)

During the second half of 1993 and from day one of 1994 I was involved in the most intense warfare against Asian strongmen. I do not exaggerate when I say I was hit so many times that each time I fell under the assault I got up thinking that it may be the last time I could survive. I had to proclaim Micah 7:8 with a resolution I felt that I did not possess.

> *'Rejoice not against me, O mine enemy: when I fall I shall arise; when I sit in darkness the Lord shall be a light unto me.'*

Nahum 1:3 and 7 were also verses I needed to repeat over and again. Over and again I identified with Job, except to say that I had the temerity to consider he had probably had a much easier time than me!

I share these things to encourage you that, however hard the battle, the overcoming can be there if Jesus is. I feel too that we may indeed all have to face a testing which seems beyond endurance, but is possible with Jesus Christ.

I am a supporter of the Open Doors ministry and when I read of the sufferings endured by our brothers and sisters in Christ, many of them are without the Word of God; boiled in oil, crucified upside-down, tortured and starved to death, I realise we are having a bit of a picnic here. The sharing of their plight through the Open Doors magazine is a quick fix for self-pity, I can tell you.

When I think of all those Bibles gathering dust in safe homes or maybe only opened briefly on a Sunday, whilst our brothers and sisters out in those unfriendly countries are clamouring to own one page, I could be sick with shame.

If one thing seems incredible to me when I reflect on the horrors of those times it is this, that God spoke to me concerning His people in the midst of it all. Does not the Bible tell us that we sow in tears and reap in joy?

> *'They that sow in tears shall reap in joy. He that goeth forth and weepeth, bearing precious seed, shall doubtless come again with rejoicing, bringing his sheaves with him.'* (Psalm 126:5–6)

Well, I have surely done both, and had the joyful witness of hundreds released, set free from the curse of treachery and betrayal. I have been so blessed as I have seen the enemy put to flight, for treachery has a most crippling effect on the body and the spirit as we see from the way victims of ME (Myalgic Encephalomyelitis) suffer.

So in January 1994 when I was groaning in the spirit for my own situation the Holy Spirit directed my heart cries to be for my fellowship Sozo Ministries. I found myself praying urgently for them on many occasions.

I was receiving that something like the sword of Damocles was hanging over the Ministry. (Damocles was once a powerful orator in Sicily invited to a feast by the tyrant elder of the island and seated under a naked sword, hung by a single thread from the ceiling, to show how precarious was the position of men in power!) Knowing the reality that Satan gives his undivided attention to where work is being done for the Kingdom, and observing the harvest and restoration of God's people at Sozo, I knew how much the enemy would like to mess it up.

The Lord awoke me many times to pray and I began to carry a burden of intense magnitude for the

Body at Romsey. I had no idea that, as in my own ministry, terrible treachery had indeed come upon them a few months previously. This was dealt with and overcome to some extent and the Body survived. But I want to explain that there are seeds of betrayal which can be left embedded in any Body of the Lord's people at such times, just waiting to ripen and grow and put down deep and evil roots of bitterness at a later date.

I hope to show you that we all, myself included, have seeds of betrayal in us if we don't watch out, and especially if we have been betrayed ourselves. The human response to betrayal is to betray. We are children of God and of course should not respond in this way of the flesh, but it is a fact of life that unless we are rigourously pursuing holiness we have a tendency in such a direction. I know, I've been there some fifteen years ago, and it resulted in the most awful torment. I praise the Lord that I was set free and have been, as a result, able to minister to others in this area.

On February 13th 1994, after having been awake in the early hours of the morning praying for my fellowship, I found myself scribbling away on my bedside notepad what I was receiving. It was like the sounding of the shofar!

I let it go as I travelled to the assembly that Sunday afternoon. Our service is from 2:30 pm to 6.00 pm at least. Upon arrival I found I could not chat to people as I normally would, and I hurridly wrote on a card a word that I had received for Sozo which was extremely urgent. My Pastor received it and put it in her Bible saying that she would take it to the Lord.

I had also been given a vision of myself ministering

to the Body at Sozo with my Pastor, her family who head up the ministry, and the leadership team all assembled in the Body as one. I was shown what I would say and do and that virtually all those gathered would respond, save about 6–10 for whom I got the word 'sprinkling'. I was shown that others would be there by divine appointment, some who travelled for healing from afar as many do. I cannot recall if I shared the vision at the time. I certainly shared it later.

Now at this time my stomach started to swell. I actually looked pregnant. I felt that I was birthing something. Then, so as not to appear super-spiritual, I examined my diet, my allergies and considered the stress I was undergoing, to off-load this 'baby' in another direction. My stomach would not deflate even with fasting, and I felt quite irritated and ungainly with the sight of it!

I continued to pray into the situation and wait on God for a revelation. It came on Wednesday, April 20th.

Chapter 3

The Revelation

On that Wednesday evening at 8.30 pm I washed my face, read some Scriptures over the kitchen table where Holy Commuion was to be shared, and asked my husband Jason to anoint my head with olive oil, to actually pour it over my head. This he did in the name of Jesus. I proclaimed a fast for victory, simply that. I knew it was not a total or even a Daniel fast. Although I would not be eating much as such, I felt no actual restriction on food from the Lord, but a time of closeness to Him and His Word.

I covered my head with a white cotton square and went to bed with a towel on my pillow because of the vast quantity of oil in my hair. As I lay in my bed I commenced to lift up and pray for all the team, intercessors and their families, and Marion and Sozo, and to bless everyone I could think to bless.

Before I commenced my prayers, I had read Isaiah Chapters 30, 31, 32 and 33 inclusive, and been quickened in my spirit by Isaiah 33:1. The Lord kept me a long time on this verse.

> '*Woe to thee that spoilest, and thou wast not spoiled; and dealest treacherously, and they dealt not treacherously with thee! when thou shalt cease to spoil, thou shalt be spoiled; and when thou shalt make an end to deal treacherously, they shall deal treacherously with thee.*'

I was caused to read the same verse in the Amplified:

> '*Woe to you, O destroyer, you who were not yourself destroyed, who dealt treacherously though they (your victims) did not deal treacherously with you! When you have ceased to destroy, you will be destroyed, and when you have stopped dealing treacherously, they will deal treacherously with you.*'

Then, when I had come to the end of my prayers and prayed for Israel, my spirit floated to the Romsey meeting. I prayed on and on in the Spirit until I fell asleep. The check I always have, which is the Holy Spirit prompting that I'll be ill if this is not discharged, seeing I have been brooding over it for months now, was **strong**.

I had also been studying out Psalm 55:12–14:

> '*For it was not an enemy that reproached me; then I could have borne it: neither was it he that hated me that did magnify himself against me; then I would have hid myself from him; But it was thou, a man mine equal, my guide and mine acquaintance. We took sweet counsel together, and walked unto the house of God in company.*'

I had been caused to do this because Marion's mother Joan, a wise lady for the Lord, had been led to this Scripture in no uncertain manner by the Lord during her quiet time with Him. She had such a witness of urgency in her spirit that she took it to Marion, who then revealed for the first time to anyone what I had given her on February 13th. Marion felt it was absolute confirmation. Joan and I exchanged some correspondence and conversation and agreed that the Lord was really speaking urgently to us.

On Friday April 22nd, my head still oiled and covered, I read the whole of Psalm 119. I was about to say 'Amen' and take Holy Comunion when the Lord caused me to write to my Pastor with a sense of urgency. It was like a 'betray and you will be betrayed' warning for the Body.

I could see that Isaiah 33:1 meant that treachery attracts treachery from both directions, from innocent to guilty, and from guilty to innocent. It was a curse operating, a web indeed, and the curse that operated when Jesus was betrayed by **His own people** the Jews.

What in fact is the definition of treachery? *Webster's Ninth Collegiate Dictionary* defines it as:
1. Violation of allegiance or of faith and confidence,
2. An act of perfidy or treason.

Treachery is in fact the breaking of faith, allegiance or confidence. It is the violation of an allegiance built up in trust and confidence, where deep and great love and/or trust has existed between people in a variety of relationships, creating a complete loyalty in all situations.

High treason is treachery against the King. We see therefore that Jesus, King of the Jews, was a victim of high treason. Judas Iscariot was the traitor. Look at Matthew 27:11:

> *'And Jesus stood before the governor: and the governor asked him, saying, Art thou the King of the Jews? And Jesus said unto him, Thou sayest.'*

Now read Matthew 24:23–25. Pontius Pilate is clearly very concerned that Jesus, an innocent man, should die such a vile death.

> *'And the governor said, Why, what evil hath he done? But they cried out the more, saying, Let him be crucified. When Pilate saw that he could prevail nothing, but that rather a tumult was made, he took water, and washed his hands before the multitude, saying, I am innocent of the blood of this just person: see ye to it. Then answered all the people, and said, His blood be on us, and on our children.'*

His murderers set up a notice over his cross, Matthew 27:37:

> *'And set up over his head his accusation written THIS IS JESUS THE KING OF THE JEWS.'*

The Jews publicly spoke a curse over themselves in verse 25:

> *'His blood be on us and our children.'*

32

This proclamation of destruction was in fact an invitation to Satan, as are all spoken curses. Looking at the history of the Jews, could we not agree that throughout history they have been constantly betrayed, both as individuals, and as a nation – hounded, betrayed, even by each other, in ghettos and other situations, unto death? Almost always horrible death. Throughout history we can see that curse being worked out over and over and over again.

The Judas spirit is one which betrays a close companion, a best friend. If a person is called 'a Judas', betrayal always comes immediately to mind. Treachery other than high treason can take place in so many areas. For example, between best friends, between spouses, between parents and children, between employer and employee working in trust together. Between doctor and patient, pastor and member of the congregation, between church leaders and their pastor, between members of committees where confidences are shared and trust is expected. Between classmates, between cell mates, between members of any group or team who would be expected to support one another. In many close-knit situations where friendship has been relied on as the guarantee for loyalty. The list is endless, the opportunities for betrayal are endless.

What is more, when such treacheries take place all manner of bad seed is sprouted. The seed of revenge or 'getting even', betraying that person who has betrayed you. The seed of unforgiveness which leads to torment. See Matthew 18:32–35.

Then there is a sin of keeping a record of wrongs, totting up in the memory, remembering all that a person has said or done against you. When they do it again, the poisons already in the mind concerning the crime or offences previously committed cause an explosion because you are reacting to the accumulation of all that has been said or done to hurt you before, and not just the incident at the time.

Friends, I have to say to you that whilst this situation of recording wrongs persists, you are as good as dead! Certainly you will never be healed of sickness, rather you will get worse, and sickness may compile upon sickness, and I know because I have been there.

The Word of God tells us that love does not keep a record of wrongs. You cannot afford the luxury of compiling lists in your mind, even as a safeguard against further betrayal. Please hear what I am saying. It does not matter what evil has befallen you, forgiveness involves **forgetting absolutely**.

Don't tell yourself it would be wise to remember or recall what someone did, just in case they do it again. Your safeguard is in total forgiveness, your release is in total forgiveness, your vindication is in total forgiveness, your overcoming is in total forgiveness, your victory is in total forgiveness. Hallelujah, praise the Lord!

Trust the Lord to vindicate you, Romans 12:17–21:

> *'Recompense to no man evil for evil. Provide things honest in the sight of all men. If it be possible, as much as lieth in you, live peaceably with all men. Dearly beloved, avenge not yourselves, but rather give place unto (God's) wrath; for it is written, Vengeance is mine: I will repay, saith the Lord.'*

God isn't saying that a person who has wronged you will go unpunished, He is saying please leave it to Me, do not interfere.

When we ask someone to state our case or defend us in a court of law we have to sit back and leave it to our barrister or lawyer to present our case in the best possible way, so that the judge can reach his verdict. We employ the best person we can for the task, and trust them to make a better job of it than we ever could ourselves.

Once we have made a decision to use a lawyer, the process of law is set in motion and we cannot bypass the lawyer or barrister to get at the judge. If we interfere with the authority of either the lawyer or judge the whole case and verdict can be confused and messed up. The situation is untenable.

One obviously does not employ a lawyer one does not trust, or we feel is not friendly towards us, having our best interests at heart. The whole business revolves around trust or it cannot get off the ground.

If Jesus is your advocate (lawyer), sitting at the right hand of the Father to intercede for you, do you trust Him to make a better job of it than you can? Is a verdict made by God ever wrong? We cannot get to the Father except through Jesus Christ. The Bible makes that so clear in John 14:6.

> *'Jesus saith unto him, I am the way, the truth and the life: no man cometh unto the Father, but by me.'*

Then there is the glorious promise in Hebrews 7:25,

'Wherefore he is able also to save them to the uttermost that come unto God by him, seeing he ever liveth to make intercession for them.'

Read also Romans 8:34. If Jesus, your lawyer, can save you to the uttermost, what more do you need? There is nothing more utter than uttermost!

Many years ago, I recall being incensed by the fact that a man of God, my Pastor at the time no less, had betrayed me, and written a lie about me which I could prove. I had 100% evidence of false accusation against me and papers to prove it.

So in the flesh I set out my 'without prejudice' case. The Bible makes it clear about not rushing to the courts against a member of the Body, but I thought in the flesh I'd just set the matter down and send him a copy so that he knew what I could prove.

When I look back at the flesh in me then I am aghast. Praise God for my sister Clare. I telephoned her and read out my epistle of complaint and asked her opinion because I knew she would be totally honest. Her response took me aback as she replied,

'It's a really exellent letter, it takes care of everything but if I were you I would tear it up and leave it to Jesus.'

I knew instantly that she was 100% correct. There was no debating. I received the truth, and it set me free. It ended months of the feeling of need of self-justification. What a blessing to have such people alongside you in the battle.

As I knelt and released the whole matter to Jesus, telling Him plainly that I was sure He could make a much better job of it than I, I knew that I was moving into a new spiritual position to deal with the Accuser of the Brethren. I never looked back and I would heartily recommend this scriptural approach to such problems!

Let us look at the Scriptures Proverbs 10:2 and 1 Peter 4:8:

> *'Hatred stirreth up strifes: but love covereth all sins.'*

> *'And above all things have fervent charity* (love) *among yourselves; for charity shall cover the multitude of sins.'*

To cover is to hide. Once it can be grasped that to have something clearly etched on the memory is **not** to have it concealed, but instead be there as a regular reminder and torment, revealed as a perpetual memorial to **sin** and **hurt**, we are definitely on our way to cleansing and healing.

Look, I have ministered to millionaires and paupers, people of different ages, colour, duration of walking in Christ, etc, and to be honest virtually all of them have had to dispense with some cruel memories. A young woman dying of a malignancy responded to me, in answer to my question, 'Have you forgiven everyone?' with, 'Well I always say I have, but I do remember what they have done when I see them.'

I want to make you a promise. As you forgive and make a quality decision to forget, you actually cannot recall what people did, and you can feel a renewed love for them.

Now please listen to what I am saying. There are times when God moves us on or away from certain people for His purposes, and indeed for our own spiritual growth's sake, but when we see them in the street or in the assembly it does not mean that we ignore them or dodge them in the car park.

The Father promises to forgive and remember our sin no more. You can do the same.

> *'And they shall teach no more every man his neighbour, and every man his brother, saying, Know the Lord: for they shall all know me, from the least of them unto the greatest of them, saith the Lord: for I will forgive their iniquity, and I will remember their sin no more.'*
>
> (Jeremiah 31:34)

Jesus says in Isaiah 43:25:

> *'I, even I, am he that blotteth out thy transgressions for mine own sake, and will not remember thy sins.'*

To blot out means to erase completely, nothing more and nothing less!

Chapter 4

The Curse of Treachery and Betrayal Explained

I continued to prepare in the Spirit to birth something! I was pregnant with it and it was like a phantom pregnancy.

I was uncomfortably heavy and very physically swollen. Yes, I had prayer for it but nothing happened. I think we all knew we were barking up the wrong tree when I fasted and it worsened, rather than improved, which indicated that food allergy which can cause such distension of the abdomen was not the cause.

Finally I felt I had almost to learn to live with it. I was certainly in travail for my Pastor and the precious fellowship. Jason left for Malaysia on May 11th, leaving me 'holding the baby', as it were. I had not shared with him my pain for the Church.

Towards the end of May my Pastor rang me with the request that I should minister to herself, her family who head up the ministry, and the leadership. We discussed what her mother had received and, believe me, Joan is no grey-haired lady quietly knitting socks, but a firebrand for Christ who runs off Satan at every turn with the blood of Jesus.

George and Joan, Marion's precious parents, run the bookshop for Sozo Ministries International and they are a force that Satan has to reckon with. Other family members are involved on the bookstall, and I always felt a great sense of delight to see this large family so united for Christ. Brother Alan does all the recording and such unity in families brings incredible strength.

We've seen it in other anointed families like Bill Subritsky's and Barry Smith's. To have each family member united in their stand against Satan is something he loathes and fears. Satan will go all out to attack such families and to destroy relationships because of the strength they have to combat him and all his works.

That is why it is important to get the whole household saved. The enemy cannot prevail ultimately against such unity. So keep on praying for your unsaved loved ones.

You don't know how to do it? Well, use this prayer from one of our Clinic prayer sheets. Put it in your Bible, insert the correct name and pray it daily. It is not confined to use for relatives of course, anyone the Lord lays on your heart.

A Prayer for Salvation

If your husband, wife, child, parent, or loved one needs Jesus, now is the time to apply your faith on their behalf. Here is a sample prayer for your unsaved loved ones. As you speak God's Word, remember that it will not return to Him void. It will prosper in the thing whereto it is sent (Isaiah 55:11).

40

'Father, I come before you in prayer and in faith, believing. Your Word says that you desire all men to be saved and come into the knowledge of the truth, so I bring _____ before you this day.

I break the power of Satan from his assignments and activities in _____'s life in the name of Jesus. Now while Satan is bound, I ask that you send forth the perfect labourers to share the Good News of the Gospel in such a way that he/she will listen and understand it. As the truth is ministered, I believe _____ will come to his/her senses and come out of the snare of the devil and make Jesus the Lord of his/her life.

Father, I ask that you fill _____ with the knowledge of Your will in all wisdom and spiritual understanding. As I intercede in his/her behalf, I believe that the power of the Holy Spirit is activated, and from this moment on, I shall praise and thank You for _____'s salvation.

I am confident that You are alert and active, watching over Your Word to perform it. It will not return to You void. It will accomplish that which You please and prosper in the thing whereto it was sent.

Therefore, my confession of faith is, God has begun a good work in _____'s life. He will perform it and bring it to full completion until the day of Jesus Christ, in Jesus' name.'

(Scripture references from the Amplified Bible: 2 Peter 3:9; Mattthew 18:18, 9:38; 2 Timothy 2:26; Jeremiah 1:12; Isaiah 55:11; Philippians 1:6.)

Isaiah 49:25 is particularly applicable to the salvation of your children:

> *'Thus saith the Lord, even the captives of the mighty shall be taken away, and the prey of the terible shall be delivered: for I will contend with him that contendeth with thee, and I will save thy children.'*

(*Note:* All our prayer sheets are available for 35p each, plus A4 SAE with 25p 1st class and 19p second class.)

My Pastor asked me if I would pray at the next Romsey Sozo Fellowship meeting for herself, her family, the leadership team and those going to minister in Scotland for the first time.

Now this was not exactly what the Holy Spirit had shown me. I believed I had heard to minister to all those persons assembled with them, with the whole Body, plus visitors, some of whom the Lord showed me would be there by divine appointment. I was to bring the Word from the platform with everyone else as the Body of Christ together in the assembly.

I would not disobey my Pastor, I love her too much, so I gently mentioned what the Spirit had shown me. She pointed out quite correctly that people come from all over the country for healing, some travelling in wheelchairs and much discomfort (I have even seen makeshift beds arrive), and that this was the Sozo service to the Body. Those arriving would not expect the usual service to be displaced by the ministry being ministered to themselves. But Marion sensed my concern and said we would have to see how the

Holy Spirit led on the day. That was very warming to me.

A lovely Christian couple, very old friends in Jesus, came to visit me a few days before the 19th of May. My husband was in Malaysia and I could not afford to telephone him, so I felt I needed prayer this end.

When I look back and see how the Spirit moved me I am amazed, although I shouldn't be. I felt to kneel down and confess and repent my own sins of recording wrongs which I had in my mind filed and computed during the awful battles with my beloved Jason, who was still affected by Hinduism and the Chinese Dragon at the time.

I told God that I suspected I had the garbage of unforgiveness to be disposed of. I had spoken out forgiveness but I was not sure if I was being honest with myself. I prayed for quite a time. I poured out a lot of junk stored in my mind and memory. Dan then prayed and we agreed that the Holy Spirit would lead Marion, and if I had heard correctly from Him then Marion would do the same. I said 'Amen' to all that and felt such a peace.

I drove to Sozo on May 29th in exceeding great joy. I sang in the Spirit and in the car Maria Callas had nothing on me! My Holy Spirit utterances were interspersed with a song the Holy Spirit gave me. I sang it vibrantly.

'Behold, I will do a new thing, and it shall spring forth. Shall ye not know it?'

Much later I discovered that was from Isaiah 43:19. Over and again I sang those words.

Most of my team were away that weekend and I knew finally that I had to go only with Jesus and the Holy Spirit to Sozo. They were my travelling companions for sure.

However, I arrived to be met by Brother Tony Teagle. Both Tony and I both needed to dive for the loo on arrival, but I suggested we had quickly to find a seat up front somewhere. I saw that virtually every seat had something on it to reserve it or someone sitting there, and then spotted two end seats in the centre block at the end of the row. I darted ahead of Tony and placed my Bible and briefcase on one of the seats. As I did a familiar voice said, 'Hello, I wondered if you would be here.'

It was my prayer warrior Marilyn, who had travelled a long way! I rarely inform her on events, she just prays faithfully and has done so for ten years. I gasped, 'Marilyn, I didn't know you were coming.'

'Neither did I,' she responded.

I knew they were God's provision and I now had both sexes from my own ministry helpers to stand with me. I quickly shared events and the meeting got under way with the usual Holy Spirit-drenched worship, which may last over an hour.

Marion brought a word on prophecy, people's thirst for it above the Word of God, false prophecy, fleeces and visions and the unreliability of much of it. It was, like all her addresses, excellent and on target. She concluded that having said all that, if a word or a prophecy was brought to Sozo they were duty-bound to check it out. She reported on the word I brought on 13/2/94 and said she believed it was a prophetic word, and a very urgent one, which was agreed by all concerned.

Now I had no idea of the details of the potential treachery looming over the ministry. I am pleased I didn't. I did know some of the history of the former betrayal, which was so similar to what happened to me because I had been sent an angel of light, a viper, into my bosom.

I did not need to know details because I knew I was under the anointing. It was extremely strong, as it has been subsequently each time I have brought the message elsewhere. It's like I have a double portion of anointing for this message. I do believe it is so important and will liberate captives in churches by the million if they will receive it.

Joan and I were both called up. Joan read Psalm 55:12–14 and explained how she received it in her prayer time. She brought it in tears and I could see many moved to tears, sensing the Spirit on her as she spoke. Those verses to me are agonising words.

Marion invited me to share how I had brought the word to her in February, and what I felt the Lord was saying. Praise God, I could see the assembly was intent on listening to every word, as they had listened to Joan.

I addressed the body, explaining fully events as they had transpired. I then asked them to listen carefully with their spiritual ears to all the questions I would be asking in the name of Jesus. I spoke as follows:

The Address

'The Lord has shown me the roots of betrayal or treachery.

"And then shall many be offended, and shall betray one another, and shall hate one another."
(Matthew 24:10)

The root of betrayal is **offence**. In Matthew 18:7 Jesus said:

"Woe unto the world because of offences! for it must needs be that offences come; but woe to that man by whom the offence cometh!"

When I say that betrayal is the Judas spirit, every Bible reader knows that I do not refer to any other than Judas Iscariot, whom Satan entered on the night of the Passover. Remember, Jesus chose the twelve apostles:

"Jesus answered them, Have not I chosen you twelve, and one of you is a devil?" (John 6:70)

I had chosen in the past a team, and one of them had a demon and what happened was horrific, but I actually chose them.

Judas had followed Jesus, listened to Him, sat at his feet. Judas was a chosen apostle, he preached the Word, healed the sick and was numbered with the twelve. He was a friend who became a foe. He was an apostle who became an apostate. In John 13:18 we read the agonising words of Jesus:

"I speak not of you all: I know whom I have chosen; but that the scripture may be fulfilled, He that eateth bread with me hath lifted up his heel

46

against me" (meaning: turned his back and walked away from Me).

Also, you will remember that Simon Peter asked Jesus who would betray Him and He replied:

"He it is, to whom I shall give a sop, when I have dipped it. And when he had dipped the sop, he gave it to Judas Iscariot, the son of Simon. And after the sop Satan entered into him. Then said Jesus unto him. That thou doest, do quickly."
(John 13:26–27)

And later Jesus, when speaking to Simon Peter in response to his protests that he would lay his life down for Jesus, replied:

"Wilt thou lay down thy life for my sake? Verily, verily I say unto thee, The cock shall not crow, till thou hast denied me thrice."   (John 13:38)

This was a betrayal twice on that night, and He knew it. In John 13:34 Jesus speaks of:

"A new commandment I give unto you, That ye love one another; as I have loved you, that ye also love one another."

The Bible is full of scriptures on love. *"Love never fails." "Faith, hope and love, and the greatest of these is love." "Love covers a multitude of sin,"* and so on. If you are filled with Jesus' love, you neither give, nor do you take, offence. Please hear what I am saying. Offence means "stumbling block". **The offence you** *take* will be *your* stumbling block. Proverbs 18:19 describes an offended person:

> *"A brother offended is harder to be won than a strong city; and their contentions are like the bars of a castle."*

An offended person is a hurting person, a person often with hatred, revenge and unforgiveness in their heart, however cleverly concealed by Satan, who blinds eyes and deafens ears so that people cannot detect their own faults. The name of the game is self-deception.

> *"The heart is deceitful above all things, and desperately wicked: who can know it?"*
>
> (Jeremiah 17:9)

Proverbs 27:6 says the kiss of the enemy is deceitful,

> *"Faithful are the wounds of a friend, but the kisses of an enemy are deceitful."*

If in your heart you would be quite pleased to see a person who has harmed or hurt you get their "just desserts", then you have unforgiveness, offence, betrayal in your heart. Offence is **sin**.

Cain's problem was offence. He was offended because his offering was rejected. He was jealous that God blessed Abel's offering. Jealousy is a root of betrayal. Joseph's brothers were jealous of their father's love and preference for him, so they betrayed him.

Many of the Body of Christ, alas, have seeds of betrayal in their hearts because they feel someone was given the job they were meant to do or more suited to. It may be playing an instrument, or being chosen to lead the Sunday School, read the lesson, or head up a prayer group. Someone may feel "I'd be better at that" or "It's my job." Bless those who have been chosen in preference to you, and praise God for them.

You also may not forgive God for an unfulfilled prophecy over your life. If the prophecy was from Him, and not of the flesh, remember that almighty God is never wrong, but promises may tarry, that the vision is for the appointed time, and that your own disobedience may be holding up the fulfilling of the prophecy. The disobedience of your spouse may be holding up the blessings for you both. Pray for your spouse, that their eyes may be opened to the cause of the stagnation and the withholding of God's blessings.

Forgive and bless them, repent before God and do not leave your Church, your fellowship or any other group offended, because overnight you could become one betrayed or a betrayer. Confess the sin of offence. The Lord taught his disciples to pray *"forgive us our trespasses as we forgive those who trespass against us."* Do that now, and ask God for mercy and forgiveness after your confession and repentance, and *"bring forth fruit worthy of repentance"* (Luke 3:8). The sign of repentance is fruit.

Remember, the greater the pruning the more luscious the fruit. Allow yourself to be pruned for His glory, and if you feel hard done by, that you are not appreciated at your workplace, or you are not in the position where you ought to be in servanthood in the

Body, that you are not being paid enough, and that you are worth much more than you are getting, resolve that offence by declaring, "I will do it all as unto the Lord."

Finally, in Matthew 26:31b Jesus said on the night that he was betrayed:

> *"All ye shall be offended because of me this night."'*

Following this description and explanation of treachery. I continued to address those gathered as follows:

'Now I am going to ask you some questions and I want you to pay attention to everything that I am saying so that you can decide if you are a candidate to be set free.

I believe that the Lord would say to you that many of you here gathered are under the curse of treachery and betrayal which is the Judas spirit.

The definition of treachery is betrayal by one to whom there is an allegiance, where trust and total loyalty have been built up and expected. It is like high treason, when a courtier close to the King betrays him, or Judas betraying King Jesus, with whom he shared food, fellowship, love, and by whom he was taught.

> *"He that dippeth his hand with me in the dish, the same shall betray me."* (Matthew 26:23)

Examine your heart and call to remembrance therefore:

Did you have a special friend in school, a best friend who deserted you for another?

If so and it broke your heart, you may be under the curse of treachery.

Did all your special relationships fall to the ground?

If so, you may be under the curse of treachery.

Did your husband desert you for another when you cherished him? Did your wife desert you for another when you cherished her?

If so you may be under the curse of treachery.

Did your best friend steal your wife or husband?

If so you may be under the curse of treachery.

Did someone dip their hand in the dish with you, eat at your table and then speak falsely against you and accuse you?

If so you may be under the curse of treachery.

Did someone you led to Christ betray you? Did you minister love and healing to another and see the power of the risen Christ raise them up, only to learn later that they betrayed and spoke falsely against you? That happened to me several times.

If so you may be under the curse of treachery.

Did you come against any of the anointed people of the Lord, although in your heart you may have had no desire to do so?

Then you may be under the curse of treachery.

Did you render evil for good, did someone render you evil for the good that you did for them, when you had taken them in and bound up their wounds?

If so you may be under the curse of treachery.

Did you labour faithfully for an employer, only to be set aside for cheaper labour?

Then you may be under the curse of treachery.

Did you lie to save your own skin and injure

another person? Did someone lie about you to save their own skin? Did you attach blame to another and see an innocent accused? Were you accused when totally innocent?

Then you may be under the curse of treachery.

Examine your hearts and your minds and your motives therefore before God. Confess, renounce and repent quietly to Him anything on your heart, anything the Holy Spirit reveals, and step forward if you feel you fit into either category, that of the betrayer or the betrayed.

The Lord will honour your confession and He will heal your wounds this day. He will set you free and cleanse you from guilt if you feel guilty, and break the curse of treachery over your life, and deliver you from the spirit executing the curse of treachery. For every curse there is a spirit that executes that curse. Then you can be cut loose from the tentacles of the Accuser of the Brethren and bless those who despitefully use you, that the Lord may reward thee as it is written.

So I leave that with you in the name of Jesus and if you feel to have this broken over you, please come forward.'

Chapter 5

Breaking the Curse of Treachery and Betrayal

The Spirit of the Lord was truly upon me as I made the altar call. Marion invited anyone to feel free to respond, including visitors. Her mother was still on the platform with us. She spoke to me very quietly.

'Do you mind if we go down below with the rest?'

My heart leapt for joy. As the Body moved into position up front I felt to ask my Pastor to anoint me with oil, which she did, and then left the platform to be with the assembly. Whilst those gathered were still coming forward I expressed my delight that everything the Holy Spirit had shown me was happening before my eyes. In a packed hall only about ten persons remained seated.

Frankly, I never saw a people so eager to receive, so intently listening to every word both Marion and I spoke. So with my Pastor, the family, the leadership team, the fellowship and the visitors up front exactly as the Spirit had shown me, I prayed.

I have had to take the prayer from the tape, because one cannot recall what one has done under the anointing. This extract from the meeting is on the cassette 'Treachery and Betrayal', available from either Sozo or ourselves. It is Part II of the 29/5/94 Romsey meeting (£3.50 including postage and packing). Much of the preceding chapter is also on the same cassette.

I explained that firstly I was to decommission an Angel of Light which I had discerned was placed in the Body, and that I had had this same awful experience. I remarked on the graciousness of God who lets what happens to us be of service to others, and that we were seeing this being worked out at that moment.

Declaring the Sovereignty of Jesus in my life and thanking the Holy Spirit for being with us, I proceeded with thanks to God and under the authority of Jesus Christ as follows:

> 'I now decommission the activity of every Angel of Light over Marion Daniel, her family and Sozo Ministries in the name of Jesus. In the name of Jesus I cut them off from this Angel of Light, and I cut them off from every harassing spirit in the mighty name of Jesus Christ of Nazareth, the name at which every knee shall bow and every tongue confess that He is Lord.
>
> I now decommission the activity in every viper's nest, right now the eggs waiting to be hatched. I come against them with the three witnesses, the Spirit, the water and the blood (2 John 5:6–8), and I render their operations null and void. I decommission every activity coming right now against this Body and against their Pastor Marion Daniel. In Jesus' name, I cut them loose from the tentacles of the Accuser of the Brethren.

In the mighty name of Jesus Christ I now break the curse of treachery and betrayal over every one of you standing here. In Jesus' name I break it, and I bind and cast out, in the mighty name of Jesus Christ, the spirit which executes the curse of treachery over all of these lives. Be bound and go down and return to the place where Jesus will send you, never more to return, never more to return in Jesus' name.

In Jesus' name, I claim the blood over Marion Daniel, her family, the leadership team and the Body here present. I put the blood of Jesus Christ between them and every accuser, and I break the teeth in the mouth of the serpent in Jesus' name.

I seal up the mouth of the slanderers and the gossips and the critical, in Jesus' name. You foul mouths, be sealed and shut up in the name of Jesus.

I declare that no weapon that is formed against Marion Daniel and Sozo Ministries shall prosper, and every tongue that rises in criticism or judgement against them will be shown to be in the wrong, because this is their inheritance, as your children, Oh Lord, and their righteousness comes from You, according to Your word.

Thank You, Father, that You will hold them up with the right hand of Your righteousness and all those who are incensed against them will be brought to nought. They will be as nothing, as a non-existent thing, for You, their Lord, have said "I will hold up your right hand with the right hand of My righteousness!"

Receive this all in Jesus' name. I speak this as

a finished work, in His name. Lord, we glorify Your name, we praise Your name and we worship You for what has been done here today, and we declare it as a finished work.'

I then invited everyone to pray in the Spirit to birth what I had prayed.

I confess it was a most moving time, and a humbling experience for me to be used as the instrument for His glory. The fervour with which every person prayed illustrated their deep commitment to one another and their understanding of the seriousness of it all.

The praise and thanks which followed must have melted the Lord's heart, as it did mine. Everyone raised their hands and declared their freedom from the curse of treachery and betrayal.

I then announced that my husband Jason had been covering me from Penang at that time, that he too had been a victim of treachery and betrayal, and that I was to join him in Malaysia within a few days.

Little did I know the vision I was to have on my way home from that meeting, for what happened at Sozo was just a forerunner of what was to come.

Chapter 6

The Vision

En route home from that deeply moving time at Sozo, as one may imagine, I was singing in the Spirit and basking in the sheer delight of so many captives set free.

It was quite extraordinary. Several dear brothers and sisters came and asked my forgiveness. In most cases I had no idea what they were talking about! That did not matter, the Spirit had moved them and I felt such love for them.

A gentleman approached me and said he had only been coming every six months, because he travelled from a long distance, but the Lord had told him to come. He told me he had been set free on this day, his birthday, of a terrible betrayal by his father. He also said a peculiar thing.

'I heard you bring a word when I came six months ago. I went home and prayed, "Lord, please let someone there bring a word on treachery."'

Several people said that they experienced an extraordinary lifting of their spirits. People from other congregations were to mention that same lightness later on.

During my time of elated praise and basking in God's love on the way home I saw a picture of myself in the sea off Penang Island, where I was baptised. Either side of me were the two Pastors who baptised me.

'What are you saying, Lord?' I asked.

It was quite amazing, because I was going to join my husband in Penang very unexpectedly. I had no idea why initially, but to confirm that I must go the same thing happened as has happened at least six times during my visits there over a decade. Someone gave me the fares! This time, when I asked why they had done so, they said that they felt I should join Jason in Penang. So I had the very definite idea that it was to see my husband who had actually gone out in order, amongst other things, to forgive the Church for betraying him! It is so incredible really how the Lord works.

As the vision continued getting sharper and not disappearing as I drove, I realised I was receiving that I must take the message on Treachery and Betrayal to the Church in Penang.

'Why, Lord?'

I felt to ask, and I sensed the Lord telling me it was there that the ministry God gave me had commenced in a special way.

'What if they don't receive it, Lord?'

I asked in my spirit, and was informed that it was not my problem, my action was to obey! It is always a lovely and reassuring feeling that all we ever have to do in such circumstances is to obey, and we do not have to be concerned with results.

Another word kept going through my mind. It was the word 'Tabernacle', an unusual word to keep popping into one's mind. I wondered if I was to take the word to a Church with the name Tabernacle in it. I knew a Church called Emmanuel Tabernacle, so my flesh wondered if that was it. Then my husband told me that someone from the Church of that name had expressed a real interest that I should do my teaching on deliverance ministry there, if I would let them know when I could come and how long I would stay.

The details of my trip at that time were a little vague as I was listening to the Holy Spirit for every step I took. I thought that if I wrote a letter acknowledging their interest and it was not of God they would not reply. I did so and did not hear a word until after I got home.

The Church which benefited from the virtually identical ministry that took place at Sozo did have the word Tabernacle in its title, and the Church which opened its door to the ministry in Penang this time was another Church with Tabernacle in its title. So that word 'Tabernacle' surely was from God, but we have to wait patiently always and not to guess.

The incredible speed with which I left for Penang was unique. Normally it would take six months to organise the Clinic, but in ten days I was on the plane heading for Kuala Lumpur! This, in spite of the fact that my cleaner/caretaker was retiring that week, and Ruth, my secretary, was nearly on her back with a painful and mysterious injury to her hip and spine. A severe nerve pain assailed her every movement. She is also my Personal Assistant and holds so many Clinic operations together it was impossible to survive in the natural without her.

I knew I had to be away for a month. What on earth would happen to the garden, the Clinic, the pile of letters arriving daily, not to mention the patients? To confirm that my journey was of Him, He undertook everything as my Jehovah Jireh yet again.

My friends Don and Pat recently back from South Africa, were resident in Birmingham and looking for a home locally. They agreed, bless them, to mind the Clinic, which would reduce the mileage for their house-hunting. What is more, Pat said she would caretake the Clinic for a month and that is no small undertaking, believe me, especially with the garden, and all the pots and flower baskets to be nurtured in dry weather!

Henrietta was thrown in at the deep end to be responsible for patients and dear Lesley, who had worked at the Clinic before, took over the reception helped by Pat. Everyone coped magnificently and they all enjoyed wonderful fellowship together. I had such a peace too that I knew the Lord was behind it all. What is more, the flight was the cheapest fare to Kuala Lumpur I had ever known in ten years travelling there, praise His name!

When Jason rang me to say he was homeward bound he was quite shocked to hear me say, 'No you're not, the Lord is sending me to Malaysia with a word for the Church. Please find us somewhere to live, and we shall need a car.'

At the time Jason, having visited his family on the mainland to sort out the grievance with his brothers, was staying with John and Annette, the former house mother and father of Goshen, the drug rehab attached to the Church where Jason was in charge for some time. This very special and anointed couple have blessed me continually with their love over some eight years that I have known them.

As soon as I arrived and recovered, we assembled our Malaysian Team and met regularly to warfare, to praise and worship and to wait on God. Sometimes we were together from 7.00 pm to the small hours of the morning. In Malaysia things get sort of timeless after midnight.

So many extraordinary things happened in our gatherings. Each and every dear brother and sister in Christ was very anointed. They were all sold out to Jesus Christ and nothing else mattered to them except serving the Lord. Time did not concern them, obedience and servanthood did.

Their love also for Jason and me was very tangible. I was constantly ministered to by their love and support, and as we pushed back the powers of darkness I saw their joy and refreshing as much as I experienced my own. Such people sadly are often left unnoticed on the fringes of the Body because of their lack of finances. Yet here is the pure gold and holiness that makes me want to weep. No wonder the Lord caused me to wash their feet. I will come back to that.

We had a lot of repenting to do, not only for ourselves but for the Church generally. I explained that we had to shoulder the repentance like Daniel did, as though it were our own sin. This so strengthened us not only as the Body but spiritually, and we watched God open doors and close doors as He willed.

Every day I kept re-reading Exodus 23:20–25, which I had received from the Lord in England before I left:

'Behold, I send an Angel before thee, to keep thee in the way, and to bring thee into the place which I have prepared. Beware of him, and obey his voice, provoke him not; for he will not pardon your transgressions: for my name is in him. But if thou shalt indeed obey his voice, and do all that I speak; then I will be an enemy unto thine enemies, and an adversary unto thine adversaries. For mine Angel shall go before thee and bring thee in unto the Amorites, and the Hittites, and the Perizzites, and the Canaanites, and the Hivites, and the Jebusites: and I will cut them off. Thou shalt not bow down to their gods, nor serve them, nor do after their works: but thou shalt utterly overthrow them, and quite break down their images. And ye shall serve the Lord your God, and he shall bless thy bread, and thy water; and I will take sickness away from the midst of thee.'

I do not believe that in all my walk with the Lord I have ever felt so submissive, so aware not to put a foot wrong as during this time. I found myself humbled under His almighty hand, and so trusting Him for each step along the way that every attack upon me rolled off like the proverbial water off a duck's back.

I received visions and Scriptures and words so clearly and so rapidly that even I was astonished. One string of words perpetually heard in my spirit was, 'Like the deaf adder that stoppeth her ear.'

I knew it was for the Church and imagine my delight when those words were traced to Psalm 58:4, the exact words. I knew it was from God because I received the word 'stoppeth' and not 'stopped'.

On the first evening we met to say hello again. These people are some of the former fruit which are abiding in the Vine. I would have thought, with the exception of two or three newcomers, there was little I did not know about them. I could not have been more wrong!

As I shared the actual recording of the ministry to Sozo tears fell, tears really fell. In some cases they washed the marble floors almost in a ceaseless stream. Sealed over but unhealed wounds were opened by the lance of the Holy Spirit. Pain was everywhere, such pain. And these dear brothers and sisters were joyful, smiling servants of God!

As I ministered into their pain and needs and the Lord set them free, I could not help wondering how many more there were out there. I suspected the numbers were millions in the Church. Soldiers of Christ dying inside, laughing outside, involved in the brave covering up of sores and agonies, going about their daily tasks with masks on! Oh, I had been there. I knew.

After the meeting in which I had delivered this word at Sozo, Pastor Marion unexpectedly anointed me for a ministry to Asians, which she said she had received for me two years previously! All those present when I played the Treachery/Betrayal cassette agreed that the message was awesome and of great consequence to the Church. They confirmed for me that my arrival in Penang was of God. I trusted their confirmation.

Chapter 7

Sharing

Each time we met to pray I was astonished how little I
had to prepare beforehand. I waited upon God, He
enlightened me as to what I was to share and teach or
minister.

I found myself amazed at what I was receiving.
Powerful instruction on the daily need for the Lord's
prayer, putting on the whole armour of God, and
proclaiming the blood Scriptures. The emphasis was
on **daily**, not upon when there was a crisis or need!

And yes, these were a praying people, people who
interceded before the throne of God, had endless quiet
times, who fasted. Yet the Lord's prayer was very
irregularly used in all cases, the armour rarely put on
afresh daily. The blood Scriptures, well-taught at the
Church they attended, were a little more used yet still
not daily. Moreover, the meetings in our flat were just
the barometer of what I found at every single place,
large or small, where I spoke.

The Lord told me to teach those matters everywhere I went as keys to survival, pointing out that in
the Lord's prayer, which was for daily bread not

monthly supplies, the words *'lead us not into temptation'* embraced a facet of treachery: the temptation to betray in end times to save our own skin!

Likewise, I had to explain that any soldier worth his salt put on new armour to go to battle in, and that we Christians could dent our armour daily even by bad thoughts about, or intentions towards, another.

Soldiers at action stations do not take their boots off, except to clean them! Often they sleep in them if trouble is looming. The boots of some soldiers of Christ are pushed so far under their beds that they could not find them in a hurry!

In Ephesians 6:11–17 where the instructions are for putting on the whole armour of God, we read in verse 11 about standing *'against the wiles of the Devil'* if we do this. Since Satan is always on the job and never deserts his post, why should we take a chance and leave the armour off or keep on the dented armour where his fiery darts may pierce? It just doesn't make sense.

Derek Prince Ministries produced a proclamation of the blood Scriptures which we find helpful:

'By This I Overcome the Devil:

> *"They* (the believers on earth) *overcame him* (Satan) *by the blood of the Lamb* (Jesus Christ) *and by the word of their testimony.* (That is, they testified to what the Word of God says about the blood of Jesus.)" (Revelation 12:11)

> *"In whom we have redemption through his blood, the **forgiveness** of sins, according to the riches of his grace."* (Ephesians 1:7)

*"Let the **redeemed** of the Lord say so, whom he hath redeemed from the hand of the enemy."*
(Psalm 107:2)

*"But if we walk in the light, as he is in the light, we have fellowship one with another, and the blood of Jesus Christ his Son **cleanseth** us from all sin."*
(1 John 1:7)

"Much more then, now ***justified*** by his blood, we shall be saved from wrath through him."
(Romans 5:9)

*"Wherefore Jesus also, that he might **sanctify** the people with his own blood, suffered without the gate."*
(Hebrews 13:12)

*"What? Know ye not that your body is the **temple** of the Holy Ghost, which is in you, which ye have of God, and ye are not your own? For ye are bought with a price. Therefore glorify God in your body, and in your spirit, which are God's."*
(1 Corinthians 6:19–20)

I testify to Satan personally as to what the word says the blood does for me:

Through the blood of Jesus I am redeemed out of the hand of the devil.

Through the blood of Jesus all my sins are forgiven.

The blood of Jesus Christ, God's Son, continually cleanses me from all sin.

Through the blood of Jesus I am justified, made righteous, "just-as-if-I'd" never sinned.

Through the blood of Jesus I am sanctified, made holy, set apart to God.

My body is a temple of the Holy Spirit, redeemed, cleansed by the blood of Jesus.

Satan has no place in me, no power over me through the blood of Jesus.'

(see footnote)

Somebody once suggested to me that my doing all this was a ritual. Well, I proved that the greatest attacks upon me were when I omitted to say the Lord's prayer, put on the whole armour of God and repeat the blood Scriptures. So through devastating experience I'd rather be ritualistic, folks!

Everything I taught those precious people was received and acted upon with great obedience and they began to gather together people who needed to hear what I was teaching and the message on treachery and betrayal. Peoples' homes and our flat started to assemble those whom God planned to receive the message before it was preached in the Church. So many were set free, it must have delighted the Lord's heart.

One sister in particular was a lovely Tamil lady with three absolutely handsome children. She had been

Footnote:
Tape No. 1018 – *Spiritual Weapons: The Blood, The Word, Our Testimony* and Tape No. 4005 – *God's Atomic Weapons: The Blood of Jesus* are available from: Derek Prince Ministries, PO Box 169, Enfield, EN3 6PL, UK.

suddenly deserted by her spouse. She used to play the guitar in worship but the moment her husband left her it was as though she died. As she lay on the floor rivers of water poured from her eyes. I also ministered against the betrayal to her three lovely children, who of course were betrayed by their father. Apparently when I left this sister took up the guitar and played for the first time since that happened, and her faith in Christ was restored.

Another man to whom the Lord spoke prophetically through me was healed of sorrow and betrayal by his Church. He had built up a ministry to the deaf and dumb and it had been snatched away and given to a professional! I knew nothing about any person in that gathering but as I heard so many loud 'Amens' I knew quite definitely that the Holy Spirit was leading and guiding me.

I want also to mention the incredible night when the Lord caused me to wash the feet of what I called the 'Malaysian Team'. Having told the Lord we had no bowls or buckets for feet, I shared with Jason the instructions I was receiving. He fetched from the kitchen the wok balanced in the frying pan, filled with water!

I washed their feet, anointed their heads and blessed each one as instructed, and this included Jason. There began a silent weeping in each and every one. The husband of one dear sister told me her husband had wept only twice in thirty-three years, when his father died and his dog died! This dear man wept for hours.

Nobody seemed to make a noise, rivers of water just poured from their eyes continuously and for a very long time indeed. Not a word was spoken except my blessing over them as I anointed each one, with the exception of Annette who kept saying, 'This is biblical.'

The next day she was given Zechariah 14:20:

> *'In that day shall there be upon the bells of the horses, **holiness unto the Lord**; and the pots in the Lord's house shall be like the bowls before the altar.'*

We broke bread together after the foot-washing and anointing, and it was as though we were sealed together for some purpose of the Lord. It was as though here was a team identical to those treasured ones at home.

How I longed for them all to meet. I knew they would all love one another, and I am believing for some millionaire in the Body of Christ to make it possible before the Lord returns! Our fellowship was sweet like nectar, and it was a powerful thrust of the Sword of the Spirit against the enemy on that troubled Island of a thousand temples and shrines.

One night as we waited upon the Lord together He instructed me to prepare to teach them about how to pray for the Jews and show them mercy. I jotted down the message as led by the Holy Spirit and decided I would try it out in a cell group where about thirty would be expected to gather.

Again I was suprised at the almost total ignorance concerning the need to pray for God's people and also of Jewish history. In case you too are ignorant, dear reader, I am going to bring the message on 'How to Pray for the Jews and Show Them Mercy', just as though you were sitting in a congregation where I was teaching this word.

It was in fact later my great privilege to bring this word as the Sunday morning message in a lovely Assemblies of God Church in a very demonic area of Penang, and the warfare prior to my bringing it should have come as no surprise!

It was as though every alternate building in that busy market town resting at the foot of the hills was a temple, shrine or very definite demonic stronghold. As we drove through the densely packed market streets to the Church we could feel the resentment in the heavenlies from principalities and powers. Jason, who was my chauffeur throughout, said he felt as though the car was being pushed. I was thankful for the prayer warriors in the car with us as we forced a passageway through the jostling throng of folks buying everything from beads to bullocks!

Chapter 8

How to Pray For and Show Mercy to the Jews

(Message as at Air Hittam, Penang, 10.4.94)

Before you read this Chapter please settle yourself quietly where you cannot be interrupted, and listen with your spiritual ears as you receive this vital message which is a key to survival in end times. Ask the Holy Spirit to quicken your godly receptors in every sense. Please get your Bibles out.

You will see that this Chapter is also to do with betrayal. Turn to John 4:22.

> '*Ye worship ye know not what: we know what we worship: for salvation is of the Jews.*'

By 'ye' Jesus was referring to the Samaritans and by 'we' He was referring to the Jews. He spoke as one of them. He spoke as a Jew. Turn to Revelation 5:5.

> '*And one of the elders saith unto me, Weep not: behold, the Lion of the tribe of Judah, the Root of*

David, hath prevailed to open the book, and to loose the seven seals thereof.'

The name 'Jew' is taken from the word 'Judah'. It is very important for us to understand the way in which Jesus totally identified with the Jews. This identification is confirmed in Scripture after His death, burial and resurrection and into eternity.

Jesus said to the Samaritan woman, as above, *'salvation is of the Jews.'* Without the Jews we would have no patriarchs, no prophets, no apostles, no Saviour and indeed no salvation. Whatever our nationality we all owe a spiritual debt to the Jews that cannot be calculated. Turn to Romans 11:30–31.

'For as ye in times past have not believed God, yet have now obtained mercy through their unbelief: Even so have these also now not believed, that through your mercy they also may obtain mercy.'

Paul here sums up what he has been saying about the debt and the responsibility of the Gentile Christians towards Israel. In other words, because of the mercy of God that has come to us as Gentile Christians through Israel, God requires us to show them mercy. How can we do this?

Firstly, remember the prophet and intercessor Daniel who set himself to pray three times a day with his window open towards Jerusalem. Daniel's prayer really disturbed Satan and threatened his satanic kingdom, so much so that he used the jealousy of evil men to bring about a change in the law that would make Daniel's prayers illegal. Nevertheless, Daniel preferred the lion's den than to cease praying (Daniel

74

6). He emerged protected by God to continue praying for Jerusalem.

I suspect in days to come such restriction will be put on our public prayers, and owning certain versions of the Holy Bible will not be permitted. There will undoubtedly be the publication and popularity of a New Age Bible which will fit all creeds, religions and denominations. It will undoubtedly be a nice comfortable tome omitting the wrath of God and the blood of Jesus!

It will aim to get rid of the victorious power of God's true scriptural word. Proclaiming His word is like using the rod of Moses. It brings about God's sovereign authority and purposes in a situation, progressively defeating all opposition, whether natural, human or satanic. Regular and confident proclamation of the Scriptures God gives us for any situation, with thanksgiving and praise in faith even before the outcome is seen, is a powerful weapon in bringing them about (Isaiah 55).

During a time of intense spiritual warfare affecting the Clinic and ministry as well as myself, God caused me to proclaim Isaiah 62, the whole Chapter, daily from a high window in the Clinic. It is a beautiful promise by God to redeem Jerusalem and Zion, but I could not comprehend why it had to be on a particular side when the room is double-aspect. I learned later that this side faces the mosque! Islamic proclamations go out from mosques five times a day, producing anti-Christ strongholds in the surrounding area, which God's word alone can defeat!

Please turn to Psalm 122:6, which is an exhortation and promise of blessing if we pray for the Jews.

> '*Pray for the peace of Jerusalem: they shall prosper that love thee.*'

Psalm 125:3a is a proclamation we can make for Israel:

> '*For the sceptre of the wicked will not remain over the land allotted to the righteous.*' (NIV)

Psalm 137:5–6 contains the Lord's own proclamation to Israel,

> '*If I forget thee, O Jerusalem, let my right hand forget her cunning. If I do not remember thee let my tongue cleave to the roof of my mouth; if I prefer not Jerusalem above my chief joy.*'

God actually tells His people to put Him in remembrance of His promises and to plead together with Him for their justification (Isaiah 43:26).

If you could proclaim such verses of Scripture daily for Israel and the Jews you could change the situation in the Middle East, and God has given us a powerful incentive to do so. Look at God's promise in Genesis 12:3 concerning showing mercy, starting with Israel:

> '*And I will bless them that bless thee, and curse him that curseth thee; and in thee shall all families of the earth be blessed.*'

Turn to Romans 11:11:

> '*I say then, Have they stumbled that they should fall? God forbid: but rather through their fall*

76

salvation is come unto the Gentiles, for to provoke them to jealousy.'

This is a second significant way in which we can repay our debts to the Jews, by demonstrating the abundance of God's blessing to us through Christ, that they might be jealous and desire what we are enjoying for themselves.

These blessings should be seen in every area of our lives, spiritual, physical, financial, material, but above all they should see and witness our pure joy in a life of righteousness, led by the Holy Spirit.

'Having then gifts differing according to the grace that is given to us, whether prophecy, let us prophesy according to the proportion of faith; Or ministry, let us wait on our ministering; or he that teacheth, on teaching; Or he that exhorteth, on exhortation; he that giveth, let him do it with simplicity; he that ruleth, with diligence; he that sheweth mercy, with cheerfulness . . . '

(Romans 12:6–8ff.)

I believe that showing mercy to the Jews both for individuals and nations will bring blessing and rescue. Few Gentiles are aware of how much we have persecuted, betrayed and hounded the Jews. The most consistent cruelty and persecution has come from the Gentiles, alas.

Historically the Crusaders, on their way through Europe to liberate the Holy Land, massacred hundreds and thousands of men, women and children. Later when they captured Jerusalem they shed more blood and displayed more cruelty than all of

Jerusalem's previous conquerors, except perhaps the Romans under Titus.

This was all done in the name of Jesus! The cross as their sacred emblem was blazoned on their banners and shields. Please never present the gospel under any title which includes or carries the word **crusade**. This word is very offensive to the Jews.

'Onward Christian Soldiers' indeed sums up a horror for many. I dislike that hymn intensely for what it portrays. Did you as a child think that the Crusaders were goodies? I did. This is quite untrue for they were indeed baddies!

In ghettos in Europe and Russia Christian priests led mobs against Jewish communities, pillaging, raping, burning and committing all manner of atrocities against them. Their justification for this was that the Jews murdered Jesus (whereas the Jews demanded His death but the Romans carried it out, including **both** Jews and Gentiles in the guilt of deicide, as do the sins of all which He took). How many of you know all this? I have found that great ignorance of such facts of history exists, both in my own country and abroad.

Then we had the systematic extermination of six million Jews in concentration camps in Europe. The instruments of this genocide were professing Christians, mainly Lutheran and Roman Catholics. Hitler himself was a practising Roman Catholic. I also find that amazingly few people know that Hitler was religious!

Furthermore, no major Christian group in Europe or elsewhere raised their voices in protest against Nazi policies. Multitudes of Christians will stand condemned in the last days by their silence, their sin of omission. To undo all this, your constant prayers and intercession are needed for the Jews, betrayed by humanity itself. Acts of collective and individual restoration are needed to restore what the locust has eaten away in persecution, torture, murder, starvation, brutality, loss of property, homes and dignity.

This is a tough message. Receive it in the name of our Lord Jesus, for we need to realise that a major factor in God's judgement of all nations will be their treatment of the Jews.

> *'When the Son of man shall come in his glory, and all the holy angels with him, then shall he sit upon the throne of his glory: And before him shall be gathered all nations: and he shall separate them one from another, as a shepherd divideth his sheep from the goats: And he shall set the sheep on his right hand, but the goats on the left. Then shall the King say unto them on his right hand, Come, ye blessed of my Father, inherit the kingdom prepared for you from the foundation of the world...'* (Matthew 25:31–34ff.)

The nations of this earth at the end of this age will be separated into sheep and goat nations and arraigned before Him for judgement. The sheep will be accepted into the Kingdom and the goats rejected, precisely on the basis of our treatment of the Jews:

> *'inasmuch as ye have done it* (ministered, or not) *unto one of the least of these My brethren ye have done it* (or not) *unto Me.'* (Matthew 25:40, 45)

In a measure some of that judgement has already taken place. For example, Britain emerged victorious from two world wars retaining intact an Empire, probably the greatest in the world. However, in 1945–1948 as the mandatory power in Palestine, Britain opposed and attempted to thwart the rebirth of Israel as a sovereign nation with her own State. From that moment onwards the decline and disintegration of the British Empire followed so rapidly that it cannot be accounted for by political or economic factors alone. More recently, Margaret Thatcher also fell from her position as Prime Minsiter and senior statesperson of Europe not long after her Foreign Secretary, Douglas Hurd, began supporting a peace treaty between Israel and the PLO. Today Britain, my own dear country (and I am patriotic) which was once Great Britain, is sadly fading into insignificance in the eyes of the world.

Again, look at the unprecedented rise in appalling violence, earthquakes and fires as a result of riots or environmental disturbance, and all manner of calamities including loss of face which followed the United States of America being unwilling even to stand security for loans to Israel to accommodate the recent Exodus, amongst other factors.

Isaiah 60:12 is an awesome proclamation of the word of God in which the Lord makes His judgement on such things plain,

> *'For the nation and kingdom that will not serve thee shall perish; yea, those nations shall be utterly wasted.'*

Please also read Isaiah 60:13–22, and then look back at Genesis 12:3:

'And I will bless them that bless thee, and curse them that curseth thee: and in thee shall all families of the earth be blessed.'

If you can, also read the Chapters in my previous books *Fruit Abiding in the Vine* and *The Anointing Breaks the Yoke*, entitled 'Weeping for Jerusalem' and 'Still Weeping for Jerusalem'. God caused me to tithe to His people and gave me an individual Jewish couple in the Alyia to bless when I can. Ask Him to lead you to prayer and to an individual Jew to assist.

The Bible is full of 'hearkens'. Hearken means to listen and obey. Please read the Scriptures I have given you carefully and bless this betrayed and betraying people. Repent for them and love them with an everlasting love, as He has. If you find this difficult, as even He has done, pray for His help!

Ask God to convict you of any personal sin against the Jewish people. A close relative of mine always called all Jews 'Shylock'. I had to repent of that for my dead relative. Shakespeare has a lot to answer for!

Someone told me that when we have a particular burden fall on us to pray for Israel, it can mean we are Jewish. My ancestors appear to be Roman Jews! As mentioned in an earlier book, I started to ask questions about this when a Messianic Jew brought his sick wife to the Clinic for treatment. As he was leaving he stuck his head back through the door and said, 'You'd better check out your ancestry, and I think you'll find you are one of us.'

Well, I did to the utmost of my ability, and it looks as if I do have a Jewish ancestry. Certainly I have been a victim of treachery many times over, and I got myself cut free of the curse of anti-Semitism when someone I trusted discerned it.

Incredibly, both my secretary and my personal assistant in the Clinic are of definite Jewish ancestry, and I don't think that is a coincidence. Likewise, there seems a real possiblity that my husband may be as well. This again was discerned by a man I trust who has a prophetic ministry and much insight into Jewish history. When we were in Israel Jason was often taken for being Jewish, and when he sings Jewish songs, accompanying himself on the guitar, I find it difficult to conceive that he isn't Jewish.

I would just like to mention, as the ministry the Lord has given me is deliverance, that all Jews and those of Jewish ancestry need to be cut free from the curse of betrayal, treachery and also the curse of anti-Semitism. Added to this, apart from cutting them off from obvious curses of starvation (which can cause over-eating and rapid eating), and also various ghetto spirits and concentration camps, there is a prevalent spirit affecting Jewish persons which may manifest in asthma.

It is the curse of suffocation and asphyxiation. I discerned this in a curious way. A sister came to me after a horrible event during a visit to Oxford. She was sitting in a cafe with her husband when she felt as though she were being strangled and choked. She was a former asthma sufferer, cured by dietary adjustment.

She had to leave the cafe for the cloakroom to avoid passing out at the table. She did not want her husband to sense her distress. However, she could not recover and had to return to the table and tell him she could not finish the meal. This upset her because they were not too well off and this was a treat for them given by a relative.

They asked me for help and I said I would be led by the Spirit. Nothing happened that day. One Sunday at the Clinic after fellowship with half a dozen Christian friends, the Lord brought this to mind and I unexpectedly started to minister to my friend.

As I prayed I saw a single railway track, quite straight, no curves, going to a building like a huge shed. I suddenly realised I was seeing a railway track which took people in trucks to the gas chamber! At that time I had not known that my friend's grandmother was Jewish.

I found myself cutting her off from the curse of Dachau, Auschwitz and Belsen as well as death. I then came against the spirit of suffocation. As I did, the Lord showed me the place in Oxford where Ridley and Lattimer were burned at the stake (near to which the cafe was located). There surely was a territorial spirit of suffocation over Oxford. Men who died at the stake must have suffocated.

Was there a transference of spirits from that place to my friend, who had this weakness because of her past asthma? And was the fact that her ancestors perished in gas chambers the reason why she nearly died on the dentist's chair, as a small child, from gas poisoning? Incidentally, I did not know of that fact until after the ministry, the fruit of which was so evident we all rejoiced and praised God.

This lovely lass got roses in her cheeks, never before seen. She ceased being constantly tired, and instead of often looking half-dead and half-asleep, she became a very vibrant and energetic young woman.

We gave God all the glory for the revelation He

gave me that day, and for His precious gift of the discernment of spirits. Praise His holy and glorious name!

Chapter 9

Offences, Over-sensitivity, Childishness in the Body of Christ

Although what I am going to bring to your attention now may seem to be a separate issue, it is part and parcel of the same problem of treachery and betrayal rampant in our midst.

Treachery and betrayal are end time entities, at least partially responsible for the divisions we see in the Church. It is not a sweeping statement I am making, nor is it an unfounded assertion, but it is based on a very wide field of experience over a decade of counselling, ministry and physical treatment of those with infirmity in the Body of Christ.

There is a *status quo* existing in so many of our churches, which I feel is not pleasing to the Lord. It is the 'them' and 'us' situation which separates the haves and the have nots, the rich from the poor. It would appear the norm for the affluent to be sitting on the Church councils or taking leadership positions in the Body, while the poor are not infrequently excluded. Jesus said that the poor would always be with us, so why not use them in high places to bless the Body? I'm not saying this applies in every Church but that my personal witness is that it is a common state of affairs.

This often leads to division within the Body of Christ, and to all manner of frustration, resentment, disappointment and even carefully concealed anger! Satan is overjoyed to see division in our Churches. Division has many tentacles and these tentacles reach out into sore areas of over-sensitivity and childishness in a manner which has so many ramifications that it's almost impossible to calculate them all. I will try to elaborate what I mean.

Jealousy, childishness, over-sensitivity and resentment are some of the roots of treachery and betrayal. They are all locked into unforgiveness. Actually this too is a hard message, but it is an evil network of sin we are looking at, and all those four tendencies can masquerade so as to be acceptable in certain cases. For example, resentment can be considered justifiable in cases of extreme hurt, and over-sensitivity thought to be excusable in cases of deep rejection.

I do bring this message in the deep love of Jesus because I want you to know, if you do not know already, that I have suffered from all these four conditions, and have overcome them one by one over some fifty years. The last fifteen years of my life, although very, very tough in so many areas, have been the happiest of my life, because I am an overcomer in Christ Jesus, having learned to refuse rejection as it is a sin!

You see, my beloved, the Holy Bible tells us that we are accepted, not rejected, and no situation, however terrible, budges us from that truth. It is that truth which sets me free and it is walking in that truth **daily** which will keep you free.

Fiery darts may come, but just put up the shield of faith to divert them! If the Father is with you, who can be against you (Romans 8:31)? Recognise that He is your Father, and that He can take care of your enemies if you are obedient to His word and do **not** interfere with His doing so (Romans 12:19)! He may not do things exactly as you wish, but His ways are not our ways, as it is written in Isaiah 55.

Turn now to 1 Corinthians 13:11:

> *'When I was a child, I spake as a child, I understood as a child, I thought as a child: but when I became a man I put away childish things.'*

I want to just bring in here that in Asian communities there may be a particular childishness, or stunting of spiritual growth, that has an unsuspected root which was revealed to me by Holy Ghost revelation during the terrible warfare I encountered in dealing with Hinduism and Chinese worship of the Dragon.

It is extremely common in Asian communities for babies and small children to be dedicated in infancy, if not at birth, in Temples or other places to the Dragon, to all manner of false gods, idols and deities. The innocent children have absolutely no choice, it is part of Asian culture. Children may even be given blood or potions to drink at that time. This very act of dedication by parents constitutes a betrayal, however unwitting, of the most horrendous and sinister type. Those innocent little lives are immediately in a trap, in bondage to false gods, as their ancestors have probably been.

If a child is dedicated to Satan that means he or she actually belongs to Satan. Likewise, if a child is dedicated to any false god they become, as it were, the property of that 'deity' (in truth, the demon symbolised by it), legally owned by them in the spiritual realm. This 'ownership' blights little lives and stunts their spiritual growth and maturity in an unsuspecting way. The whole evil is compounded when it has happened in generation after generation of the same blood line.

Unless the miracle of salvation occurs in these lives, they are still surrendered to such idols and have no real will of their own. They are controlled, in bondage. That control is real, it is witchcraft. Unless the soul ties with the Serpent, Dragon and every other false god are cut off at the roots, and this can only be done when idolatry in the ancestors has also been confessed, renounced and repented, their complete spiritual growth and maturity cannot take place.

There are many other reasons too, of course, for the fact that people generally in the Body of Christ may take a very long time to grow up. They are the late developers spiritually, so to speak. They react like small boys and girls to any given situation, not infrequently defending themselves when nobody is attacking them, except Satan through their minds.

Their tongues often go uncontrollably into action! Proverbs 18:21 says:

> 'Death and life are in the power of the tongue: and they that love it shall eat the fruit thereof.'

Are you eating the fruit of your tongue? We have to

realise that what we say will come to pass, and what we fear will come to pass. For example,

> *'For the thing which I greatly feared is come upon me, and that which I was afraid of is come unto me.'* (Job 3:25)

> *'O generation of vipers, how can ye, being evil, speak good things? for out of the abundance of the heart the mouth speaketh.'* (Matthew 12:34)

Are you eating the fruit of your tongue? I repeat that question. Examine your hearts now and be honest with yourself when you do.

With our tongues we can put curses upon ourselves and others with deadly effect. I speak from painful experience, having reaped a harvest of agony by cursing both my arms and my legs! If you do not know about that read my first two books published by New Wine Press, *Go and Do Likewise* and *Fruit Abiding in the Vine*.

With our tongues we can crush and destroy, or encourage and build up. I have a ministry of God today because two Pastors from Penang encouraged me that this was so. One is always led by Satan to suspect that one is imagining it. The Accuser gets very busy in this area when he sees that a ministry to glorify the Lord Jesus is blossoming and bearing fruit. I am always so grateful to God for sending men and women to encourage me.

I want you, however, to know that during these last five years when the Lord has been breaking me in one fiery trial after another, I have been able to see quite clearly that He is the only person I can trust utterly and totally. I have learned to be solely dependent on my Father, like all obedient children should be. I trust Him absolutely for every area of my life, especially direction and discernment. We, that is none of us, can actually rely on people (including ourselves!) in the sense of direction for our lives. Turn to Jeremiah 17:5:

> *'Thus saith the Lord; Cursed be the man that trusteth in man, and maketh flesh his arm, and whose heart departeth from the Lord.'*

Now let's look at the dreadful curse of barreness and wilderness that is promised if we do not rely on the Father absolutely, in verse 6:

> *'For he shall be like the heath in the desert, and shall not see when good cometh; but shall inhabit the parched places in the wilderness, in a salt land and not inhabited.'*

Then we have the blessing for obedience in verses 7 and 8:

> *'Blessed is the man that trusteth in the Lord, and whose hope the Lord is. For he shall be as a tree planted by the waters, and that spreadeth out her roots by the river, and shall not see when heat cometh, but her leaf shall be green; and shall not be careful in the year of drought, neither shall cease from yielding fruit.'*

These blessings are not for the double-minded. There are times when we all need inner healing for our deep hurts and wounded spirits. We need our wounds to be bound up in Jesus' name. But to be honest, and I know for sure that it is not only my experience in ministry but that of others, we do see that unless we speak out boldly against it, the same people come up repeatedly for prayer for the same old grievances, answering altar call after altar call for problems that should have been dealt with in the first instance.

I have to say, however, that they do not queue up for a second time on prayer lines where I am teaching this message, because I make it very clear in the name of Jesus, whose servant I am, that the word means what it says in James 1:8:

'A double-minded man is unstable in all his ways.'

Being single-minded about deliverance ministry is probably the most important aspect of it. Being single-minded, not wavering, not coming into unbelief because of Satan's tricks, by making a quality decision to grow up, is the first step to spiritual maturity. It enables you to move on in the name of Jesus Christ.

Now can we refer back to Jeremiah 17:6 where the Scripture says *'and shall not see when good cometh'*? I wish to turn to the problem, not only for all believers whose eyes Satan can blind, but specifically for Asians. It needs remembering that many Hindu and Chinese ancestors have been involved in worship of the Cobra or Dragon (two of Satan's main manifestations). Before the cobra actually strikes to kill, it blinds the eyes, which depicts exactly what Satan does. In Scripture two of the Devil's names are the

Dragon and the Serpent: Dragon as the destroyer and Serpent as the Accuser, beguiler and deceiver.

If you are an Asian with a poisonous tongue, given to gossip and criticism, it could be that ancestral Cobra worship is a root to be dealt with. Asians are not the only races to have serpentine spirits of course. Being in the presence of a person with such a spirit can also make a person feel strangled and crushed.

Our Lord and Saviour said in Exodus 3:14:

'I AM that I AM.'

He did not say 'I was that I was'. Function in the **now**! Not in the past, not in the future but in the present, in the here and now. Do not look back. Let every breath you take be Holy Ghost inspired.

The finest aid you have for this walk is **constant** reference to the Manufacturer's handbook: get into the Scriptures, I mean into the meat of the Word.

> *'For every one that useth milk is unskilful in the word of righteousness: for he is a babe. But strong meat belongeth to them that are of full age, even those who by reason of use have their senses exercised to discern both good and evil.'*
> (Hebrews 5:13–14)

One experienced estimate is that 90% or more of the Church never fully take in even the milk! This covers the first doctrines of salvation: repentance from dead works, faith toward God, baptism, laying on of hands, resurrection from the dead and eternal judgement (Hebrews 6:1–3). But if one does not get all those, and on to the meat of ever increasing discernment of good and evil, learning how to live daily in the good, in righteousness (Hebrews 5:13–14), you will never, never ever move out – or stay – in power.

This does not mean only learning the words, but constantly practising and exercising one's discernment. Only unceasing use refines and develops it. How many preachers have to report their observations that Charismatics are still the easiest to fool?

2 Timothy 2:15 and 3:16–17 say:

> *'Study to shew thyself approved unto God, a workman that needeth not to be ashamed, rightly dividing the word of truth.'*

> *'All Scripture is given by inspiration of God, and is profitable for doctrine, for reproof, for correction, for instruction in righteousness: That the man of God may be perfect, thoroughly furnished unto all good works.'*

Of course reproof, correction and instruction in righteousness have often been unpopular amongst God's people, as compared with ready acceptance by the heathen! This is a repetitive theme of Scripture, e.g. Matthew 12:41; 10:15–17, 23; Ezekiel 3:3, 14 and Revelation 10:10 describe God's prophetic words regarding judgement for disobedience as 'honey in the mouth but bitter in the belly' and spirit. It feels so right at first but can become quite bitter when fully taken in, obeyed and spoken out.

Bitter means mourning, lamentation and woe, which both Ezekiel and John prophesied would be the result of disobedience, but their words were – and will be – rejected. God had to give Ezekiel (Chapters 2 and 3) a divinely strengthened face, and forehead like flint, to withstand both words and looks like 'briars and thorns and scorpions' which he would meet from God's own 'rebellious, impudent and hardhearted' people. Nevertheless, God said He was the One who would shut and open Ezekiel's mouth, and that Ezekiel could only deliver his own soul by warning them, whether they listened or not!

Yes, the Word should cheer us, make us happy but it should also cause us to fear the Lord. Who considers the wrath of God these days? Just recently, when everyone else seemed to be laughing, I was crying! A lot of the team, unbeknown to each other, started weeping all over the place too. It was so embarrassing. None of us knew why we were doing it and it was a long time before each found out about the others.

These are all people who spend time with God and they were crying. The Lord repeatedly gave me Joel 1 at my communion table, where I am solitary with Him. Finally, I thought it must be that I had heard wrongly, but I kept on praying. Right now I have nothing in the natural to weep about, but boy can I weep! If any reader gets me a revelation on Joel 1, I'll be delighted to hear it.

Turn to 1 Timothy 4:1–2:

> 'Now the Spirit speaketh expressly, that in the latter times some shall depart from the faith, giving heed to seducing spirits and doctrines of devils; Speaking lies in hypocrisy; having their conscience seared with a hot iron.'

Just consider these words, Church. The people here referred to, departed from the faith. Some things that are happening in our Churches recently are enough to cause folks to depart from the faith!

As mentioned earlier, one of the greatest sins in the Body of Christ is over-sensitivity, and I am now going to elaborate on that particular facet of treachery and betrayal. Hear with your spiritual ears, and receive in love what I am bringing in love.

Over-sensitivity is Manipulation. It's Witchcraft, Folks! Sensitivity is a beautiful God-given aspect of our nature, as are the five senses He has given us, of **touching, smelling, seeing, hearing** and **tasting**. All of these senses can be grasped and got hold of by the Devil and distorted.

Touching can become molestation or stealing.

Smelling can become smoking, glue sniffing.

Seeing can become lust of the eyes.

Hearing can become receiving gossip or false doctrine.

Tasting can become gluttony etc., etc.

Are you over-sensitive? Be honest now, otherwise you'll not get free later on. Does your Pastor or your cell group leader have to meet your needs? Are you easily offended? Let me give you a few examples of what I mean. These are imaginary but typical conversations one hears:

'Well, my Pastor ignored me today. I smiled at him across the hall and he ignored me. I wonder what I've done?'

'Nothing actually. He was busily engrossed with the problem of Sister Beatrice, to whom he

95

was giving his undivided attention, apart from which, he cannot see long distance without his spectacles and he didn't have them on. In any event, if that had been you wanting his private attention, would you have been happy if he took his eyes off your face and smiled and waved all over the room?'

'Oooh! Jean usually takes me home in her car after Church and she didn't offer me a lift. I wonder what I've done?'

'Nothing. In fact she had to rush Sister Susie to see a friend in hospital in the opposite direction to your house, and did not have time to explain what had happened.'

'Oooh, I'm really hurting. Janet and Tom had a party and they didn't invite me. I wonder what I've done?'

'Nothing actually. They only had room for a certain number of guests and someone told them you were away that weekend.'

Are you numbered amongst the over-sensitive, the touchy ones, the easily offended? Do you pretend false guilt in such situations as I have described, to get attention?

If you walk into a crowded room and hear someone say, 'You fool,' do you think they are referring to you?

Do members of your family and fellowship have to meet your needs, do what you want or think best?

In Christ you are there to meet the needs of others, to die to self and to be healed pouring out for others

(Isaiah 58). Years ago God used to say to me when I moaned,

> 'Pour out, Pour out, pour out, even to the last drop of blood.'

That's what Jesus did for us all. I got healed by doing this, of so many things. I'm being healed right now as I write this. I get healed every time I preach these words, when I speak to my patients about such things, when I write about them in my books. We can minister to ourselves, you know. Try it sometime.

If you keep on wailing, 'Ooh! I'm still hurting, I'm still hurting,' what you are really saying is 'I'm not ready to forgive you yet.'

Well, you'd better get ready quickly and apply Matthew 18:34 or you will be delivered to the tormentor. Along with that torment will come fear. These two, fear and torment, are demonic partners in crime.

> *'Then his lord, after that he had called him, said unto him, O thou wicked servant, I forgave thee all that debt, because thou desiredst me: Shouldest not thou also have had compassion on thy fellowservant, even as I had pity on thee? And his lord was wroth, and delivered him to the tormentors, till he should pay all that was due unto him. So likewise shall my heavenly Father do also unto you, if ye from your hearts forgive not every one his brother their trespasses.'* (Matthew 18:32–5)

> *'There is no fear in love; but perfect love casteth out fear: because fear hath torment. He that feareth is not made perfect in love.'* (1 John 4:18)

Here are a few more searching questions. Answer truthfully.

When people are in your company do they have to walk on eggshells for fear of offending you? That's witchcraft, folks, controlling people with your moods, 'sending them to Coventry' if they do not meet your emotional needs.

At meal times, when a cook is offended if the food is not liked, or those being served sulk and lose their appetite if they do not receive the food they fancy, then be careful, it's witchcraft, folks, subtle manipulation. Moodiness, black sulkiness, becoming angry, ignoring people. It's witchcraft. **Beware!**

I know someone whose husband sulks, and goes off his food if he gets an omelette or fishcakes, but the sight of a sizzling joint makes him bouncy and joyful. The wife has to budget. Meat is not good for someone every day anyway.

These people are all guilty of witchcraft. It starts when children will not eat up their greens unless a piece of chocolate is on the table to bribe them. One child I know shunned everything his parents tried to tempt him with, once he heard the doctor say to the mother when he was sick, 'Let him eat what he fancies.'

He only ever fancied Marmite sandwiches and at the age of fourteen they were still his staple diet, with all the resultant symptoms of Candidosis. Children, alas, can be right little manipulators, and you must recognise that for what it is: **witchcraft**.

If your partner is around whilst reading this book, put it down and go and ask him or her sweetly, 'Darling, am I touchy? Do you have to pick the right time to say certain things to me?'

Do you ever, for any reason, ignore people in the assembly, bypass them in the aisle after the service, or look away? Do you give a 'peace of Jesus' hug in the meeting, and then become impatient or irritated afterwards when their car is blocking your exit as you wish to make a dash for the Sunday roast? If I squeeze an orange, orange juice comes out. If we are squeezed, then Jesus' love should come out!

We must ask God for daily wisdom in our speech and actions. James 1:19a says:

> 'Wherefore, my beloved brethren, let every man be swift to hear, slow to speak, slow to wrath.'

Alas, there are some folks, so touchy, so super-sensitive that we almost have to get into mind-reading to assess their reactions before we open our mouths. That is an extremely dangerous position to be in. Reading of peoples' minds borders on the occult.

All these matters need to be brought in the open in the Body of Christ and dealt with. This spiral of super-sensitivity and being easily offended, so that others have to meet your desires or emotional needs is a whirlpool of darkness.

Why? Because it totally blocks the spontaneity of the Spirit of all Truth, the Holy Spirit. You will find yourself powerless to help because that witchcraft has robbed you of the power of the spontaneity of the Holy Spirit. You have been disarmed, made impotent! I must add that if this state of affairs exists in your home it will definitely infiltrate outwards into the Body of Christ, and bring with it the Accuser of the Brethren.

Beware too of manipulative prayers, e.g:

'Dear God, will you please make my Pastor give me the job of playing the keyboard on Sunday?'

'Dear God, will you please make John marry Joan?'

'Dear God, will you make Tim leave so I have more of a chance of heading up the choir?' etc., etc., etc. (All fictitious names, of course.)

Do you know one of the most terrible things I ever heard once in a Baptist Church? The Pastor was a very handsome, personable and attractive man. He was married to a sweet lady who was really rather ill at one time. It came under discussion, can you believe it, of whom he would marry if she died! Such a shocking curse upon the Pastor's wife, almost like wishing her dead. No wonder some heathens find us not too attractive. And do not take offence because of what I say, because it could be **your** stumbling block, as it is written!

> *'Woe unto the world because of offences! for it must needs be that offences come: but woe to that man by whom the offence cometh!'*
>
> (Matthew 18:7)

Your pastor does not have to make himself a continual crutch for the lame, or they will never learn to walk solely dependent upon the Lord. That is what the aim is, folks! Your Pastor cannot carry every sheep on his shoulders but the Lord can, for the Government is on His shoulders, Halellujah!

Insecurity and lack of trust are at the root of over-sensitivity. See all these roots attaching to one another? If you are trusting God, believe me, all will be well. He says He will never leave us or forsake us:

> *'Let your conversation be without covetousness;
> and be content with such things as ye have: for he
> hath said, I will never leave thee, nor forsake
> thee.'*   (Hebrews 13:5)

The structure of the Body of Christ is founded on
trust. Mistrust provokes suspicion, attention-seeking,
insecurity, loss of confidence and over-sensitivity. All
areas are breeding grounds for offences. And if you
feel unloved, I'll give you the remedy. Try loving and
pouring out for someone else. I do not mean someone
who is loveable either, but someone who is ugly, difficult, poor, fatherless, widowed, covered in sores.
James 1:27 applies:

> *'Pure religion and undefiled before God and the
> Father is this, To visit the fatherless and widows
> in their affliction and to keep himself unspotted
> from the world.'*

Unspotted from the world includes not goggling at
the TV at the expense of Bible study. No, I'm not
going to go on about the television again. My last
three books have many chapters on its witchcraft and
manipulation, how the Lord revealed it to me as a
pagan shrine at which people are worshipping in their
sitting rooms all over the world. I actually saw the
golden bird-shaped idol, prince of the power of the
air, both in the spirit and in a dream so clearly.

You may imagine this is a tough word to bring. The
ramifications of the message are endless, but wherever
I have brought these things out into the light, congregations and assemblies have been set free. The Church
is divided, folks. It's sick, it's disobedient in many

areas, it's full of witchcraft. Jezebel reigns supreme in many cases, engaged in subtle but deadly manipulation and control, and it all needs to be dealt with so the Church can be strong and united and free. Please hear what I'm saying. We are in a warfare!

And remember too that gossip is as witchcraft. Years ago gossips would be publicly put under water on ducking stools as a punishment! Are you a Christian gossip?

For example:

> 'I'm only telling you about brother Sid, Anne, so you can pray for him.'

> 'Ooh, we are having a meeting because Ted and Jane are doing this or that, and we are all meeting to discuss how to pray for them.'

Oh, no you don't! If you have a problem with Sid, Ted or Jane you just get in the closet and pray for them. If you are critical, if you are receiving bad reports about your brothers and sisters in Christ, and sowing bad seed and discord amongst the brethren it will become a cancer in your midst. Repent and be set free in the name of Jesus Christ, who died for you and them on the cross at Calvary.

> *'Let no corrupt communication proceed out of your mouth, but that which is good to the use of edifying, that it may minister grace unto the hearers. And grieve not the holy Spirit of God, whereby ye are sealed unto the day of redemption. Let all bitterness, and wrath, and anger, and clamour, and evil speaking, be put away from you, with all malice: And be ye kind one to*

another, tenderhearted, forgiving one another, even as God for Christ's sake hath forgiven you.'
(Ephesians 4:29–32)

Please read this Chapter very carefully again before continuing the book because I hope that you will come before the Lord with confession, renunciation and repentance in all of these areas.

I delivered this message to the Church in Penang. I really believe it is a hefty message, but it was life-changing where it was received, just as it was for Sozo Ministries who were on their way to minister in Scotland, following which no less than six miracles were reported in Scotland, as well as the usual healings and deliverance. The Body at Sozo is totally transformed. People look different, are different. Below are two short extracts from letters my Pastor received following the ministry on 29th May 1994.

'...Pearl's word was such a blessing. I can't tell you how released I felt after that ministry. It was wonderful that so many people responded. It was really powerful coming forth at just the right time, being confirmed in Scripture like that. Really awesome. I don't know how others felt but I felt something really deep being released, a bit like something pulling at my insides. Praise the Lord!'
(T.A., Southampton)

'...The tape before the last one, where Pearl ... gave her word was a really good one. I listened to it on one of those horrible hot days and almost jumped from my couch when she shared about the spirit of treachery! It really was the case of the "missing key". The Lord led me to a chapter in Isaiah which confirmed what Pearl had said and last week we had a guest speaker who spoke on the same subject so the whole thing was doubly confirmed and followed up. It is wonderful to see how God provides answers to our questions...'   (T.H., Germany)

*   *   *

We acknowledge with thanks the teaching from Marion Daniel on this subject, and recommend the box of her four tapes on *Flies in the Ointment*, cost £10 plus p & p, from Sozo Books.

Chapter 10

Deliverance From Evil

I pray that you have read very carefully all the afore-said on childishness, over-sensitivity and offences in the body of Christ.

If now you feel you are childish or have a juvenile spirit, that you are a manipulator or that you are manipulated, consciously or unconsciously, or a gossip, or you are guilty of grapevine criticism, then you need to say this prayer.

What do I mean by grapevine criticism? It is criticism, bad seed about your brother or sister in Christ, passed on from mouth to mouth. You probably haven't taken what you have heard to the Lord and sought His face on it, you have probably not checked out the facts for yourself, but are parrotting the accusations of others. You probably have not allowed for those individuals having been dealt with by the Lord five minutes before **you** received the gossip! Brothers and sisters in Christ, we have **all** been there!

Examine your hearts. Have you a deep-rooted unforgiveness that causes you to mistrust and mis-construe the actions or thoughts and intentions of others? Are you easily hurt, offended and over-sensitive? Do you always blame somebody else for the condition you are in?

If so, you need to repent and call upon the Lord to set you free, so that you may grow in Him and walk in victory in every area of your life. Be excited for a finished work in your life concerning these painful matters which bring every infirmity in their wake.

> *'The Spirit of the Lord God is upon me; because the Lord hath anointed me to preach good tidings unto the meek: he hath sent me to bind up the brokenhearted, to proclaim liberty to the captives, and the opening of the prison to them that are bound.'* (Isaiah 61:1–3)

Say this prayer now to the Lord. ('I' and 'my' may be substituted by 'we' and 'our', as suitable.)

The Prayer of Repentance

Loving heavenly Father, I come to you in the name of Jesus Christ who died for me on the cross at Calvary that I might be saved, healed and whole in Him.

I confess, repent and renounce the sin of unforgiveness, of keeping in my mind a record of the wrongs done to me, of being over-sensitive and childish, of manipulating others through my moods and grievances (or allowing myself to be manipulated), of taking offence and attaching blame to others, of allowing bad memories to poison my heart and my thoughts.

Cleanse, O Lord, my mind of every painful and destructive memory. Cleanse my heart and renew a right spirit within me that I might walk free of all the sins of over-sensitivity, manipulation, taking offence and unforgiveness, and never more keep a record of wrongs, in Jesus' name I pray.

Response by Person Ministering
(or may be said by oneself)

Loving heavenly Father, you have heard the prayer of your children and Your word promises freedom to those who call upon the name of Your Son, and as your anointed representative:

I break the stronghold of over-sensitivity and unforgiveness over these members of the Body of Christ. I break the stronghold of witchcraft and manipulation in Jesus' name and I bind and cast out the spirit which executes the curse of witchcraft, in Jesus' name. You be bound and go down to the place Jesus has prepared for you, never more to return.

With the Sword of the Spirit, the word of God, I gouge out every spirit of cancer and root of criticism, I pluck it out to the deepest root of bitterness, in Jesus' holy name.

In Jesus name, I annul every ungodly covenant set up with Satan and every agreement with the Accuser of the Brethren. I cut you off from the Accuser of the Brethren and render null and void every corrupt communication that has proceeded out of your mouth or come against you, to wound, destroy or cast down.

I bind and I cast out, in Jesus' name, every foul-mouth spirit and spirit of contention and strife. Be bound and go down in Jesus' name, never more to return.

In the presence of the three witnesses, the Spirit, the water and the blood (1 John 5:6–8), I come against every word and lying tongue that has gone forth to feed the Accuser. The Lord rebuke thee, Satan, off these lives.

I make this declaration in the presence of the three witnesses, the Spirit, the water, and the blood, that you Satan have been holding these people illegally, for the price was paid on Calvary's cross, as it is written (1 Peter 2:24).

Thank you, Father, that it is written that you will forgive us our trespasses as we forgive those who trespass against us. And now I have done this in your sight and name, I loose the blessing of the Lord's forgiveness onto these people. I pronounce them free, healed and whole in the mighty name of Jesus. I declare the word of God,

'And I heard a loud voice saying in heaven, Now is come salvation, and strength, and the kingdom of our God, and the power of his Christ: for the accuser of our brethren is cast down, which accused them before our God day and night.' (Revelation 12:10)

And I proclaim that 'ye now love one another as Christ has loved you.' It is a finished work. May all the glory go to Him, hallelujah, Amen.

Now just praise and thank the Lord in your own way for setting you free. Do this every morning for at least 28 days, after which time of proclamation you will **know** how free you are.

Bless you all who have prayed this prayer or had it prayed over you. I love you and so does He! Praise His holy and merciful and gracious name. Amen.

Chapter 11

Ministry for Asians

(Africans and former non-Christians may say the same prayer)

Prior to saying this prayer, if you have already received salvation and are not in an assembly, it would be wisdom to break bread and take the cup, remembering Jesus' victory over all evil.

Opening Prayer

Loving heavenly Father, I come to you in the name of my Saviour Jesus Christ.

I confess, renounce and repent all my sins. (Name sins as the Lord convicts you, audibly but quietly to Him.)

I forgive every person who has hurt or sinned against me. Especially I forgive (name those the Lord recalls to your mind who have damaged you in any hurtful way).

I confess, renounce and repent the sins of idolatry in my life, and in the life of my ancestors and forefathers, known and unknown.

I repent of my, and their, adherence to the

guidance of mediums and the receiving of astrological prognostications over my life, and of every demonic bondage to soothsayers and medicine men, mediums and sorcerers, witchdoctors and all ungodly men and women.

I renounce the setting up and study of birth charts made over my life and over the lives of my ancestors. I rebuke their content as a lying spirit, which is cancelled out by my renunciation of all their evil assignments over my life and the lives of my ancestors.

I repent of the drinking of blood and swallowing of papers and potions of medicine men in myself and my ancestors.

I repent of cobra and all serpent worship, and the worship of animal deities and forces of air, fire, water, the nether world and nature.

Forgive me and my ancestors, O Lord, of every form of idol worship, and every past agreement with any ungodly covenant set up by Satan and his demons over our lives.

I declare the sovereignty of the Lord Jesus Christ in my life and call upon Him to set me and my ancestral line free through the confession of my faith in Him alone.

(*Note:* 'I' and 'my' may be substituted by 'we' and 'our', if applicable.)

Response by Person Ministering
(or may be said by oneself)

Lord, I come to you in the name of Jesus as your anointed representative, reminding You of Your most holy promise to set free all those who call upon Your merciful name.

In the mighty name of Jesus Christ of Nazareth, I come against every spirit and god of air, fire and water, the nether world and nature and every idol and animal deity in your lives. I break their stronghold over yourselves and your blood line back unto the first generation of idolators, and release you and your forbears from the sin of idolatry, which is cancelled and blotted out by your confession and repentance in the presence of the three witnesses, the Spirit, the water and the blood (1 John 5:5–10).

I cancel the effects of every birth chart and annul every ungodly covenant set up by Satan over your lives. I sever you from every ungodly prediction and astrological prognostication and every commitment and dedication made for you at birth or by yourself later on. I loose you from the bondage of every ungodly covenant and dedication in Jesus' holy name, for as it is written,

'Thou shalt have no other gods before me ...
thou shalt not bow down to them or worship
them.' (Exodus 20:3, 5a)

I cut every soul tie with the Dragon. I excise the claws of the Dragon, the accuser and destroyer from the flesh of all those under the sound of my voice, and I release them from the Dragon's claws, in Jesus' name.

I cut you off from the curse of the drinking of

blood, eating meat sacrificed to idols and strangled creatures. I cut you off from the drinking of medicine man or witchdoctor potions by yourself and your ancestors, and from diagnosis or foretelling by the use of bones, hair or any other ungodly tool. In Jesus' mighty name, be free!

> *'Ye are of God, little children, and have over-come them: because greater is he that is in us than he that is in the world.'* (1 John 4:4)

> *'The weapons of our warfare are not carnal, but mighty through God to the pulling down of strongholds.'* (2 Corinthians 10:4)

In Jesus' name, I now pull down the stronghold of betrayal at birth by parents, or any other person in charge of these people as infants, by the dedication to idols, in temples or any other place. I pull down, in Jesus' name, the stronghold of such dedication made by their own lips at a later age.

In Jesus' holy and mighty name, I break down the images of the false gods of these peoples and their ancestors and I utterly overthrow them, and release you from their domination and control **forever**!

In Jesus' name, I break every stronghold and fear of false gods in your lives and the lives of your ancestors. I bind and cast out the spirit of fear, and the spirit of the fear of revenge by false gods.

In Jesus' holy name, you spirits which execute the curse of fear and fear of revenge, be bound and go down, in Jesus' name, to the place that Jesus has prepared for you, **never** to return. I loose the perfect love of Jesus which casts out fear into these people under the sound of my voice. I declare that God has not given them a spirit of fear but of love and power and a sound mind (2 Timothy 1:7).

I break the curse of the insanity of ritual suicide and death, and bind and cast out the spirit which executes the curse of ritual suicide and death in these people, in Jesus' name.

I cut you off from all cobra and serpentine worship, ancestral and otherwise. I cut you off from all mesmerism, trance and hypnosis which has come in through cobra and serpent worship or any other ungodly ritual or source. I cut you off from every poisonous tongue spirit and venomous speech, in Jesus' name. I rebuke every venomous trait in yourselves and your ancestors relating to cobra, serpent or idol worship, and I sever the serpent's head with the Sword of the Spirit which is the Word of God, and render it powerless and dead in you, in Jesus' name.

In the name of the Lord Jesus, I refuse every spell, hex, voodoo or curse spoken against these people, and I say you return to the one who sent you, in Jesus' name, never more to return.

I cut you off from the spirit of **India**, and every caste spirit and curse, in Jesus' name, (or)

I cut you off from the spirit of **China** and every

provincial spirit, triad and secret society and curse, in Jesus' name, (or)

I cut you off from the spirit of **Africa** and every tribal spirit and curse, in Jesus' name.

Whatever your nationality, I cut you off from every territorial spirit and curse, and from their reign of terror over your domain. In Jesus' name, be loosed and set free, that Christ may rule and reign in your lives.

In the presence of the three witnesses, the Spirit, the water and the blood, I now rebuke the devourer in your lives, in Jesus' name. I declare that you are set free and shall serve the Lord your God with all your hearts and strength, and He will take sickness away from the midst of thee. Amen. Blessed be the name of the Lord for ever and ever, praise His holy name.

Following this prayer, praise the Lord as you are led. If you feel sleepy, do not be concerned. So much has been lifted from you that you may even have been unaware that you are carrying. The lifting of such horrendous burdens may make you feel so relaxed that you sleep as you have never slept before. Just thank God, give Jesus all the glory for what has been done and remember it no more.

All those transgressions of yourselves and your forefathers are blotted out by your confession and repentance. Do not let Satan snatch any of your freedom back through disobedience, or lack of faith in the finished work of Jesus in your lives. Many people use their Bibles as never before following such ministries. I pray that this will happen to you.

I praise God for your openness, and obedience to what He has revealed to me for you. I thank Him to be used as an instrument for His glory. Keep me humble and seeking after holiness, my Lord Jesus.

Chapter 12

Healing of ME Through Breaking the Curse of Treachery and Betrayal

Testimony of Lorraine Paige

Lorraine first came as a patient to the Clinic in March 1994 whilst I was away, before I had received all the revelations on treachery and betrayal described in this book, but her experience is such a clear example of how it may operate.

Henrietta, my assistant, took the initial consultation and on her second visit she came, as is customary, for food testing of some eighty common foods and twenty environmental allergens. Whilst upstairs being tested Henrietta received the word 'Betrayal'. I was back from my week's rest by this time, but was downstairs and knew nothing of this.

When Lorraine and her husband Phil came down, I was very taken with his godly behaviour as a husband. They were in their late twenties and early thirties and one would not have expected such spiritual maturity. I saw that Phil prayed for her and with her, that he was protective with a gentle authority. I observed later that he always carried his Bible and was very keen to be reading it.

Men who have wives suffering from ME need a patience that only God can give. I do not see a great deal of that always. Women so need cherishing at such times. I recall saying to my secretary Ruth, 'This marriage is a godly marriage.'

Ruth replied emphatically, 'Amen!'

I had no idea at the time that Lorraine and Phil had prayed that I would pray for Lorraine before she left the Clinic. Lorraine had been warned in advance of coming here, through my book *The Anointing Breaks the Yoke*, that patients cannot demand ministry because I am led by the Holy Spirit, nor can I succumb to such demands as I did once out of fleshly compassion. She totally accepted that.

As they were leaving the Holy Spirit led me simply to lay hands on her and pray in the Spirit, nothing more. I obeyed and as I prayed my right hand came out from my side as though I was patting something low down. I wondered if it was a dog. I got one word: 'Betrayal'.

Upon asking Lorraine she said she was not a victim of betrayal. I continued to pray in the Spirit and got the identical word. I questioned Lorraine again, and she told me that Henrietta got the same word. I was delighted.

I continued to pray in the Spirit, still patting this low down whatever it was with my right hand. Suddenly I discerned it was like as if I was patting the head of a small child. I confronted Lorraine with the words, 'Oh, it's a small child, you lost a best friend who betrayed you.'

Lorraine wept. I cut the soul tie with this girl and Lorraine was instantly healed of ME, just as I had been!

She is really getting stronger, cycling some miles now and learning how to eat properly, to exercise and take care of the temple of the Holy Spirit, her physical body. Even when patients are healed they are happy to do this and I know God is teaching them discipline.

Ours is not a freak diet but a food programme whereby after twenty-eight days, all being well, the body should be thoroughly detoxified of allergens and environmental toxins, after which new foods may be reintroduced. Few patients do not lose all their allergies within three months.

I will let Lorraine tell her story exactly in her own words, and we give Jesus all the glory.

'I had been ill with ME for nearly seven years when a friend, who had been treated at the Clinic (also for ME) gave me a copy of Pearl's book *The Anointing Breaks the Yoke*. I was excited and devoured it very quickly, although I hadn't been able to read properly for years.

I had been through all sorts of things with God before hearing about Pearl's work – disappointment at not being healed when I became a Christian (about 18 months into the illness), further disappointments at not being healed when I had faith to be healed, feelings of being forgotten and abandoned by God, and feeling a failure for not living in victory, and frustration at not being able to live my life fully. Through it all, however, I experienced the comfort of Jesus and knew deep in my spirit, even in my most desperate times, that He had a perfect plan for me and that I would be healed in His timing.

When I read Pearl's book I was filled with excitement and hope and wanted to go to the Clinic straight away! I made an appointment and was tested for Candidosis, which I had, and was given information about a food programme to get rid of it, and vitamins and minerals to help build up my immune system again. I didn't see Pearl on my first visit because she was away, but she was there the second time and I had more allergy testing.

My husband Phil had prayed that we wouldn't go away without having her ministry, and as we were about to leave Pearl said she felt to pray for us in the Spirit. This she did and asked if I had ever been betrayed. I had read the book and searched my past, but all I could remember was a best friend who used to bully me a bit and I didn't really think that that was a betrayal.

When Pearl asked if it was a childhood best friend, I suddenly remembered that this same friend whom I'd known since I was five had joined my tutor group in the second year of comprehensive school because she was unhappy in her own and wanted to be with me. I felt I should go around with her although I already had a friend in the group, so I gave up this friend, then my best friend deserted me for another girl in the group, leaving me to go around on my own for a long time afterwards.

This memory was very painful and I began to cry. Pearl prayed for me and broke the curse of treachery on my life and I was delivered from the spirit of infirmity. Immediately I felt alive again! It's so good to be free and I praise God for my healing and my new-found strength and life every day.

It is taking time to rebuild my strength and energy levels and my immune system but I know that the ME has completely gone, and so has the Candidosis and all the allergies which I had. I'm looking forward to finding out what the Lord wants me to do with my new life now!'

Upon reflection I saw that indeed Isaiah 33:1 applied to Lorraine, for really she had herself given up her new friend to return to her old best friend. In doing so she lost both relationships. Her new friend must also have felt betrayed when she was abandoned for Lorraine's earlier childhood best friend. There had been a real soul tie when her best friend could come and steal her away from a new pal!

Chapter 13

Angels of Light

One of the things that staggers me is how one holds fast to what the Word of God says on a certain issue, and then allows one's conceptions to be changed because somebody we deem spiritually superior, older in the Word of God shall we say, has preached something on the subject with an entirely opposite viewpoint. So it was with me a decade ago, and I do not relate this with anything but shame and to show how easy it is to be misled.

Ten years ago to be honest, I had not given angels, except the Angel of the Lord, a great deal of thought. At the time I had read, but not studied, in Hebrews concerning ministering spirits (Hebrews 1:14). Frankly, I had no desire to call upon angels since my prayers were all to the Father through Jesus Christ, my Lord and Saviour. I was very happy about that. I felt this the only secure and proper way to petition my Father in heaven (John 15:16).

In 1986 my studies of the Word started to get really serious and the more I studied, the more ignorant I found myself to be. I was ashamed of my ignorance as I had been a Christian since the age of three and spent no less than thirty-three years in one Anglican Church and seven years in another Anglican but Charismatic Church before I moved into house fellowship and then on to the Baptist Church.

On many occasions I was quite overcome by my ignorance and tended to receive what was taught by illustrious preachers, never checking out the Scriptures for accuracy myself, although I would take copious notes at lectures, seminars and conferences.

I'm sure as we are growing spiritually we all go through the stages of meetingitis! I know I was always attending something to learn more, but sadly listening to what speakers said, accepting it as truth without checking it out myself with the Word of God, confident that these 'oldies' were 'authorities' and wiser than I. More learned and expert in every way! It is all so different now, as it takes a lot for me to be led out of the closet to meetings, although some men of God whose teachings I have found sound will always draw my attention.

About eight years ago I attended a meeting at Brighton, really because so many I knew were going and I did not want to miss out! I was not into checking with the Lord what I should do in those days. It seems shocking but that's how it was then, and I am sharing this, as I share much, to enlighten readers that I have been just as foolish and ignorant as anybody.

There was a teaching at this seminar that angels were all unemployed or underemployed in the heavenlies because we were not giving them orders! I swallowed this erroneous teaching hook, line and sinker, not really studying it out. I left the conference feeling guilty, and convinced that I should give the angels a few jobs from time to time. However, I always forgot and went through Jesus Christ as before. I kept thinking, 'Oh, dear, I still haven't commanded any angels, given them any orders. There they are, sitting with their wings folded!'

There just did not seem to be any need. Then one fateful day a dear Christian friend whom I had met recently as a patient, told me that her car had got bashed a couple of times and could I pray about it.

'Ah!' I thought, 'a job for those unemployed angels.'

Well, what happened after that really confused us and should have been a warning. If my friend's car was attacked by the enemy before we prayed that, each time I gave the 'unemployed' angels a job to guard it the most awful damage to her car occurred afterwards! It was bashed en route, vandalised whilst parked outside her house, had graffiti scrawled all over it, etc., etc.

'I can't make it out,' she complained, 'every time you tell the angels to look after my car it gets more damaged. I have more accidents!'

My friend lives in a town which is laced with covens. I am sure the enemy has marked her out, yet obedience to the Word affords her a great degree of protection, even in such an area. However, I somehow didn't attach what happened to her car to my disobeying the Word of God concerning angels. I still had not checked on it because I didn't normally use the angels.

Then one fateful day I was off for my first teaching ministry to Europe. Whilst I was on the plane I thought, 'I know, I'll tell the angels to go before me.'

That was the worst thing I ever did, I can tell you.

Instead of angels going before me, someone followed me back who, wittingly or unwittingly, set out not only to divide the team but destroy the ministry as well, both at home and abroad! Only later on, after I had checked this teaching out for myself and asked a few questions about commanding angels of those I trusted from experience, did I see how much in error I had been, and repented smartly!

However, can you believe it, even after such terrible experiences and receiving the truth in my inward parts, I heard yet another minister invite us to tell the angels to do various things to assist us, because they were virtually unemployed. Goodness me, I thought temporarily. I was now newly married to Jason so I would consult him. He has done very intensive Bible study from Derek Prince's teaching and knew far more of the Word than I. He gave me an emphatic 'No' to commanding angels.

I also wrote to those Bible teachers I had learned a lot from and found very sound. I must emphasise I had ceased commanding angels and lost sight of the issue, until I suddenly heard this almost identical teaching again, that we could do so, and what is more coincidental – or was it? – a patient brought me a tape from yet another speaker who was also into commanding angels! I was certain something was going on, but I did not realise what until I got the last letter from those to whom I had written.

It came from Peter Horrobin of Ellel Ministries. He wrote:

> 'I do not believe we have any authority over Angels. The Angels are sent to help those who are receiving salvation but they are sent by the

Lord. I believe we have a right to intercede and ask God to send the Angels but it is He who chooses whether or not the Angels are sent and what they do.

I believe that if we start commanding Angels around we are out of order and we may then open ourselves to the deception of commanding demons around who will manifest as an Angel of light in order to deceive us yet further. So I agree with your discernment.'

I gasped! I finally realised without doubt that we had had an encounter with an 'angel of light', one of the satanic 'transformed ministers of righteousness' described in 2 Corinthians 11:13–15:

'For such are false apostles, deceitful workers, transforming themselves into the apostles of Christ. And no marvel: for Satan himself is transformed into an angel of light. Therefore it is no great thing if his ministers also be transformed as the ministers of righteousness; whose end shall be according to their works.'

It had been a very terrible and shaky time, but God's mercy prevailed. This person had sought to make herself indispensible to me. If anyone ever tries to convince you they are indispensible, beware witchcraft.

And if satanic personification as an angel of light sounds extreme, just recall Jesus' response to Peter, who only expressed natural human concern that his beloved Friend should not undergo terrible suffering and death.

> '... *Get thee behind me, Satan: thou art an*
> *offence unto me: for thou savourest not the things*
> *that be of God, but those that be of man!'*
>
> (Matthew 16:23)

You will recall (from the last chapter of *The Anointing Breaks The Yoke*, p. 219) that the Rev. Marion Daniel discerned I had been sent an angel of light and cut me off, as well as praying about treachery. Angels of light bring teachery of course. Marion was spot on and that deliverance, as I related, changed my life. This angel of light was a definite factor in my sickness, and a major aspect of the treachery and betrayal.

I am relating this confession of my ignorance because I have been so horrified by what has happened to people through comanding angels, and under Ezekiel 3:18–19 and 33:7–9 I have to warn them. Be warned. It is serious!

> '*When I say unto the wicked, Thou shalt surely*
> *die: and thou givest him not warning, nor speak-*
> *est to warn the wicked from his wicked way, to*
> *save his life; the same wicked man shall die in his*
> *inquity; but his blood will I require at thine hand.*
> *Yet if thou warn the wicked and he turn not from*
> *his wicked way, he shall die in his iniquity; but*
> *thou hast delivered thy soul.'*

> '*So thou, O son of man, I have set thee a watch-*
> *man unto the house of Israel: therefore thou shalt*
> *hear the word at my mouth, and warn them from*
> *me. When I say unto the wicked, O wicked man,*
> *thou shalt surely die: if thou dost not speak to*

warn the wicked man from his way, that wicked man shall die in his iniquity; but his blood will I require at thine hand. Nevertheless, if thou warn the wicked of his way to turn from it: if he do not turn from his way, he shall die in his iniquity; but thou hast delivered thy soul.'

Other comments on commanding angels are listed below. But you also check out the Scriptures now. Do **not** learn the hard way as I did!

Beryl Hunter

'Re. Angels question. Big No, No to that sermon. We cannot command angels, only God can do this (unless fallen angels and one commanding is of the enemy – these are then evil spirits). Hebrews 1:14 – This verse speaks of ministering to us as part of "drawing to salvation" – by God. *Note:* "for **them who shall be** heirs of salvation." Thereafter, angels are sent to protect, fight and minister, as part of our heavenly inheritance as "sons and daughters of the living God." They behold the glory of God; only He can direct them. They don't worship or glorify us. They worship and **obey** Him. They don't obey us, because we don't have the glorified power to command these heavenly beings.'

Bill Subritsky

'I do not find any reference in Scripture that we are entitled to command angels. Nevertheless we can ask the Lord to place angels around us for protection. Many times I get prophecies that, indeed, angels are around us. I would confine my own belief in this matter to asking the Lord to send His ministering angels in certain circumstances.'

David Noakes

'Many thanks for your letter about "commanding the angels". I believe it is yet another piece of teaching which arises out of human arrogance and a lack of proper understanding of the Word of God, and is totally wrong. Hebrews 1:6–7 – Whose angels are they? They are **God's** angels. What right have we to give them orders? Hebrews 1:14 – God **sends** them; we have no right to summon them. Hebrews 2:7 – Until we are glorified like Jesus, we are **lower** than the angels.

If people who teach this sort of nonsense really knew the Bible, they would not do it. The OT accounts of the manifestation of angels show it to be an awe-inspiring experience – e.g. Judges 6:22 and 13:6–21, Isaiah 6:2–4, Ezekiel 1, Daniel 8:15–18, etc. I am sure the hesitation which both you and Jason have is right. If we ask the Lord to send His servants, He surely will, but to think to order them about is just pride and foolish ignorance!'

John and Elsa Linden-Cook

'Agreed! We cannot command angels. But we can ask the Lord Jesus to send them to help us. He has done this for us more than once.'

Now please hear what I'm saying. We can all learn

from each others' mistakes. Do not get super-spiritual and think you cannot make one. You stand less chance if you are not lazy about listening to the Holy Spirit as well as studying the Word. I always learn things the hard way, but I seem to get there in the end through the mercy of God, praise His name.

The function of an angel of light is to deceive and confuse, to divide and destroy. Angels of light come as very attractive personages. They may even sow money into the ministry. I know of two cases where this was definitely the case. What is more, funds were really needed in those ministries so the danger was in depending on these angels of light.

How can anyone who is funding you be ruining you? Sorry folks, the answer to that is easy. Satan will use any plot or ploy to disrupt ministries bearing fruit. He has no scruples, no shred of honour, only one motivation: destruction.

Be warned. Be attentive to the Word of God. By all means let your trusted teachers bring you the Word, but check out everything for yourself. If you find you have been deceived, humble yourself under the mighty hand of God, who is swift to forgive those who truly repent, and move on in victory, praising His name.

Counterfeit is everywhere; everything of God can be counterfeited by Satan, do not forget that. Lying signs and wonders will accelerate in these end times. Get ready. Ask for the gift of the discerning of spirits, a precious weapon in these days of urgent preparation for the Lord's return. Then make sure to use it!

Please note these Scriptures, which clearly make commanding unemployed angels impossible, except in disobedience (with all its consequences):

(1) Psalm 103:20 **together with** Isaiah 55:8–9:

> *'Bless the Lord, ye his angels ... that do **His** commandments, hearkening unto the voice of **His** word ... ye ministers of **His** that do His pleasure,'*

and

> *'My thoughts are not your thoughts, neither are my ways your ways, saith the Lord. For as the heavens are higher than the earth, so are my ways higher than your ways, and my thoughts than your thoughts.'* (emphasis added)

God Himself says, first, the angels are His, they obey Him, do His commands, and second, our ways and thoughts (thus all commands produced by them) are **not** anywhere near His, so it is **impossible** for angels to obey us without disobeying Him, and if they did they would no longer be His! Jesus Himself said you **cannot** serve two masters (Matthew 6:24a).

(2) Those telling us to command angels say they are **unemployed**. However, it is also scripturally impossible for any unemployed angels to be God's. God's Word requires those of the kingdom of heaven to be continually engaged in good and fruitful works, especially to the poor and needy, and says those who are idle will be cast into the darkness and fire prepared for the devil and his angels, e.g. the parables in Matthew 25 (especially verses 30, 41).

Proverbs 19:15 and 31:27, Ecclesiastes 10:18, 1 Timothy 5:10–13 indicate idleness is an aspect of sin and corruption, like Ezekiel 16:49:

> *'Behold, this was the iniquity of thy sister Sodom, pride, fulness of bread, and abundance of idleness was in her and in her daughters, neither did she strengthen the hand of the poor and needy.'*

No Scripture says, or even implies, that heavenly angels are idle or unemployed. Many verses command us to **wait** on the Lord, e.g. Psalm 37:7, 9, and Luke 12:33–40, but this shown to be a very active and not an idle thing at all. Therefore, to say or accept angels **are** idle or unemployed is to **add** to Scripture, and so call down plagues on oneself, according to Revelation 22:18, and in fact this is just what happened!

(3) 1 Chronicles 21:18 says that *'the Angel of the Lord commanded Gad.'* To command requires superiority and authority over those commanded. The angels are shown to have this over man throughout Scripture, but could not have had if men could in fact command them.

2 Corinthians 11:13–15 says angels of light are any (human) workers, ministers of 'righteousness' or 'apostles' who are deceitful or false. These may come from outside or inside the Church (Acts 20:29–30), deliberately or innocently (Galatians 2:4), demonically (1 John 2:18–19, 4:3), or merely humanly. Jesus called Peter 'Satan' and an offence to Him for, in effect, simply thinking and reacting as a man and not God (Matthew 16:23)!

135

It is often easier to think, feel and react according to our human nature rather than the Holy Spirit, and to accept others who do, especially when it seems something nice, comforting, helpful, etc. To discern and reject as clearly Jesus did anyone speaking 'in the flesh' as man, rather than 'in the Spirit' as God, requires continuous awareness of and submission to the Word and the Holy Spirit, not to mention seeking and trusting Jesus' help to do so!

This is not something super-spiritual, but vitally practical every day. The first bit of Romans 8:1 is only true **with the rest**:

> *'There is therefore now no condemnation* (including damnation) *to them which are in Christ Jesus,* **who walk** (live, act) **not after the flesh** (human nature) **but after the Spirit.'**

> *'To be carnally* (humanly) *minded is death; but to be spiritually minded is life and peace.*
>
> *Because the carnal* (human) *mind is enmity against God; for it is not subject to the law of God, neither indeed can be!'*　　　(Romans 8:6–7)

Chapter 14

John the Baptist Was Offended

I want to put this question before you, 'Did John's offence at Jesus cost him his head?'

Think about it. Without this stumbling block, would the outcome for him have been different? At Jesus' baptism John knew without doubt that Jesus was the son of God. Read John 1:6–9, 15–18:

> *'There was a man sent from God, whose name was John. The same came for a witness, to bear witness of the Light, that all men through him might believe. He was not that Light, but was sent to bear witness of that Light. That was the true Light, which lighteth every man that cometh into the world ... John bare witness of him, and cried, saying, This was he of whom I spake. He that cometh after me is preferred before: for he was before me. And of his fulness have all we received, and grace for grace. For the law was given by Moses, but grace and truth came by Jesus Christ. No man hath seen God at any time; the only*

begotten Son, which is in the bosom of the Father, he hath declared him.'

For further clarification we read in John 1:29–36 as follows,

> *'The next day John seeth Jesus coming unto him, and saith, Behold the Lamb of God, which taketh away the sin of the world. This is He of whom I said, After me cometh a man which is preferred before me: for he was before me. And I knew him not: but that he should be made manifest to Israel, therefore am I come baptizing with water. And John bare record, saying, I saw the Spirit descending from heaven like a dove, and it abode upon him. And I knew him not: but he that sent me to baptize with water, the same said unto me, Upon whom thou shalt see the Spirit descendinq, and remaining on him, the same is he which baptizeth with the Holy Ghost, **And I saw, and bare record that this is the Son of God**. Again the next day after John stood, and two of his disciples; And looking upon Jesus as he walked, he saith, Behold the Lamb of God!'*   (emphasis added)

These Scriptures make it quite plain that there was no doubt in John the Baptist's mind who Jesus was. So what happened for him to query this fact later on? Look at Matthew 11:1–6:

> *'And it came to pass, when Jesus had made an end of commanding his twelve disciples, he departed thence to teach and to preach in their cities. Now when John had heard in the prison the works of*

> *Christ, he sent two of his disciples, And said unto him, Art thou he that should come, or do we look for another? Jesus answered and said unto them, Go and shew John **again** those things which ye do hear and see: The blind receive their sight, and the lame walk, the lepers are cleansed, and the deaf hear, the dead are raised up, and the poor have the gospel preached to them. And blessed is he, whosoever shall not be offended in me.'*

The emphasis on the word 'again' in verse 4 is mine. Jesus confirmed that John once knew the answer to his own question, from the signs and wonders he witnessed at Jesus' baptism.

Have you realised, brothers and sisters in Christ, that doubt and unbelief concerning a person or their ministry, even a perfectly godly one, may be caused by taking offence? Or how serious the consequences can be? That awesome word in Matthew 5:29–30 says it is better to cut off a part of the body which is causing us to offend, than to be cast into hell!

There is such a fine line between taking offence and judging righteous judgement. However, nowhere are we to be sloppy if we have discerned doctrines of demons. It is not only possible but vital to judge rightly, and to stand firmly against that which is not honouring to the Lord Jesus and all that was done on the cross.

> *'Now the spirit speaketh expressly, that in the latter times some shall depart from the faith, giving heed to seducing spirits, and doctrines of devils; Speaking lies in hypocrisy; having their conscience seared with a hot iron.'* (1 Timothy 4:1–2)

Remember, offence was taken against **Jesus**, the Son of God and God Himself, not only by John the Baptist before the death of Jesus but by all His apostles and disciples on the night He was betrayed, not because of anything morally wrong in Him, but because of their weaknesses, ignorance, fear, lack of faith, etc. We **are** to guard against this evil twist of human nature which Jesus called hypocrisy. Wrong reactions and judging of others due to problems in oneself is what Jesus was addressing when He said:

'Judge not that ye may not be judged.'
(Matthew 7:1a)

He was **not** referring here, as explained more fully in the next chapter, to the genuine and sincere member of the Body of Christ who truly wishes – and needs – to discern false manifestations of the Holy Spirit, false prophets and teachers, as many Scriptures exhort us do.

This is where the daily praying of the Lord's prayer is essential for every follower of Jesus Christ. We need that daily deliverance from evil, folks!

Chapter 15

Is It Right to Judge?

I have just mentioned in the previous chapter the vital necessity to judge righteously, and I was going to write more on this subject when I received an article by Dr James Van Zyl, of Faith in the Word Ministries in South Africa.

Readers may recall that I met Dr James in Jerusalem and that it was through his teaching that I began taking daily Holy Communion, and how much it blessed me. His wonderful booklets, including *The Lord's Table and Healing*, have blessed so many who sent for them. (Enquiries to PO Box 112, Stanger 4450, South Africa.)

I have received permission for the excellent truth in his article about judging to be reproduced here. I am certain that you will find it as helpful as I did.

Is It Right to Judge?
by Dr James Van Zyl

This question 'Is it right to judge?' is one that puzzles many Christians. A careful and open-minded study of the Bible makes it clear that concerning certain vital matters, it is not only right but our positive duty to judge. Many do not know that.

The Scripture Commands to Judge

The Lord Jesus commanded:

> *'Judge righteous judgment.'* (John 7:24)

He told a man,

> *'Thou hast rightly judged.'* (Luke 7:43)

To others our Lord asked,

> *'Why even of yourselves judge ye not what is right?'* (Luke 12:57)

The Apostle Paul wrote:

> *'I speak as to wise men; judge ye what I say.'* (1 Corinthians 10:15)

Again, Paul declared,

> *'He that is spiritual judgeth all things.'* (1 Corinthians 2:15)

It is our positive duty to judge.

False Teachers and False Teaching

'Beware of false prophets' (Matthew 7:15) is the warning and command of our Lord. But how could we 'beware' and how could we know they are 'false

142

prophets' if we did not judge? And what is the God-given standard by which we are to judge?

> *'To the law and to the testimony: if they speak not according to **this word**, it is because there is **no light** in them.'* (Isaiah 8:20)

'Ye shall know them by their fruits' (Matthew 7:16) Christ said. And in judging the 'fruits' one must judge by God's Word, not by what appeals to human reasoning. Many things seem good to human judgement which are false to the Word of God.

The Apostle Paul admonished believers,

> *'Now I beseech you, brethren, **mark them** which cause divisions and offences contrary to the doctrine which ye have learned; and **avoid them**. For they that are such serve not our Lord Jesus Christ, but their own belly; and by good words and fair speeches deceive the hearts of the simple.'* (Romans 16:17–18)

This apostolic command could not be obeyed were it not right to judge. God wants us to know His Word and then **test all** teachers and teaching by it.

Notice also that it is the false teachers who make the 'divisions', and not those who protest against their false teaching. And these deceivers are not serving Christ, as they profess, 'but their own belly', or their own 'bread and butter', their own aspirations and building their own kingdoms as we would put it. We are to **'mark them'** and **'avoid them'**.

> *'Come out from among them, be ye separate, saith the Lord.'* (2 Corinthians 6:17; read verses 14–18)

143

'From such turn away.' (2 Timothy 3:5)

'Withdraw yourselves.' (2 Thessalonians 3:6)

'And have no fellowship with the unfruitful works of darkness, but rather reprove them.'
(Ephesians 5:11)

'Abhor that which is evil; cleave to that which is good.' (Romans 12:9)

'Prove all things; hold fast that which is good.'
(1 Thessalonians 5:21)

It would be impossible to obey these injunctions of God's Word unless it were right to judge. And remember, nothing is 'good' in God's sight that is not true to His word.

The Apostle John wrote:

> *'Beloved, believe not every spirit, but try* (test, judge) *the spirits whether they are of God: because **many** false prophets are gone out into the world.'* (1 John 4:1)

Again he wrote,

> *'If there come any unto you, and bring not this doctrine, **receive him not** into your house, neither bid him God speed: For he that biddeth him God speed is partaker of his evil deeds.'*
(2 John 10–11)

This Scripture commands us to judge between those who do, and those who do not bring the true doctrine of Christ.

Whenever a child of God contributes to a denominational budget that supports unscriptural theologies, he is guilty before God, according to this Scripture, of bidding them godspeed in the most effective way possible. And he thereby becomes a **partaker** with them of their 'evil deeds' of spreading soul-damning poison. How terrible, but how true.

Arouse yourself, child of God. If you are guilty, ask God to forgive you and help you never again to be guilty of the blood of souls for whom Christ died. When we are willing to **suffer** for Christ, we can readily **see** the truth of God's Word on this tremendously important matter.

> *'If we suffer, we shall also reign with Him.'*
> (2 Timothy 2:12)

Misunderstood and Misused Scripture

One of the best known and most misunderstood and misapplied Scriptures is *'Judge not'* (Matthew 7:1). Let us examine the entire passage:

> *'Judge not, that ye be not judged. For with what judgement ye judge, ye shall be judged: and with what measure ye mete, it shall be measured to you again. And why beholdest thou the mote that is in thy brother's eye, but considerest not the beam that is in thine own eye? Or how wilt thou say to thy brother, Let me pull out the mote out of thine eye; and, behold, a beam is in thine own eye? **Thou hypocrite**, first cast out the beam out of thine own eye; and then shalt thou see clearly to cast out the mote out of thy brother's eye.'* (Matthew 7:1–5)

Read this again carefully. Note that it is adressed to a hypocrite! – not to those who sincerely want to discern whether a teacher or teaching is true or false to God's Word. And instead of being a prohibition against honest judgement, it is a solemn warning against hypocritical judgement. In fact, the last statement of this Scripture commands sincere judgement: *'then shall thou see clearly to cast out the mote out of thy brother's eye'*.

If we take a verse or a part of a verse out of its setting, we can make the Word of God appear to teach the very opposite of what it really does teach. And those who do this cannot escape the judgement of God for twisting His Word (2 Peter 3:16). Let this be a warning to us never again to take a text of Scripture out of context.

Many who piously quote 'Judge not' out of its connection, in order to defend that which is false to God's Word, do not see their own inconsistency in thus judging that which is untrue to the Bible. It is tragic that so much that is anti-scriptural has found undeserved shelter behind a misuse of the Scripture just quoted. The reason the professed church of Christ is today honeycombed and paralyzed by satanic modernism is because Christians have not obeyed the commands of God's Word to judge and put away and separate from false teachers and false teaching when they first appeared in their midst. Physical health is maintained by separation from disease germs.

Spiritual health is maintained by separating from germs of false doctrine. The greatest peril of our day is not too much judging, but too little judging of spiritual falsehood. God wants His children to be like the noble Bereans who *'searched the Scriptures daily, whether those things were so'* (Acts 17:11).

Romans 2:1–3 is also addressed to the religious hypocrite who condemned himself because he was guilty of the same things for which he condemned others. James 4:11–12 refers to an evil spirit of back-biting and fault-finding, not to judging whether teachers or teachings agree or disagree with God's Word. The Bible never contradicts itself. To understand one portion of Scripture we must view it in the light of all Scripture.

> *'No prophecy of the Scripture is of any private* (isolated) *interpretation.'* (2 Peter 1:20)
>
> *'Comparing spiritual things* (words) *with spiritual.'* (1 Corinthians 2:13)

The 'Wheat and Tares' parable of Matthew 13:24–30, 36–43 is much misunderstood. First of all, our Lord is talking about the world, not His Church: 'the field is the world'. He goes on to say that *'the good seed are the children of the Kingdom; but the tares are the children of the wicked one'* (Matthew 13:38). They are the two groups in the world: children of God – those who have received Christ (John 1:12), and the children of the devil – those who reject Christ (John 8:44)

When any of the 'children of the wicked one' get into the professed church of Christ, as they have always done, a definite procedure for God's children is set forth in His Word. First, it is their duty to tell them that they have 'neither part nor lot' in Christ (see Acts 8:21–23 and context). If the children of the devil do not leave voluntarily, as is generally the case, God's children are commanded to 'purge out' these unbelievers (1 Corinthians 5:7).

But God's people have disobeyed His word about this, so unbelievers have taken control, as is now the case in most denominations. Therefore those who purpose to be true to Christ and His Word are commanded to *'come out from among them, and be ye separate, saith the Lord'* (2 Corinthians 6:17), regardless of property or any other considerations. When we obey God's Word, we can trust Him to take care of all the consequences of our obedience.

Note the following: it is believed by most Christians, and often quoted from Scripture, that God never changes.

'For I am the Lord, I change not.'   (Malachi 3:6)

'Every good and every perfect gift is from above, and cometh down from the Father of lights with whom is no variableness (change) *neither shadow of turning.'*   (James 1:17)

'Jesus Christ is the same yesterday, and today, and for ever.'   (Hebrews 13:8)

Keeping these Scriptures in mind we know that God always acts in the same way, true to His character. In the Old Covenant (Testament) God sent His prophets to warn His people, but on many occasions they were scoffed at and stoned: Abraham, Jonah, Jeremiah, and many others. But God's judgment always came to pass and fell upon the wicked earth: floods, fire and brimstone.

In the New Covenant (Testament) God sent Jesus Christ, the Greatest Prophet to warn God's people and to set an example. But many, many disobeyed Him, and suffered severe consequences. There was the man in the Bible who lived with his mother as his wife whom Paul handed over to Satan for the destruction of the flesh in order that the spirit may be saved in the day of the Lord Jesus (1 Corinthians 5:5). Paul did the same with Alexander and Hymenaeus because they blasphemed (1 Timothy 1:20). Ananias and Sapphira lied to God (Acts 5) and were struck dead. These last two people were mature Christians who were supposed to know the will of God, yet they chose to sin, and judgement fell upon them.

There is no record that they were first counselled by their brothers about their sin, and secondly counselled by the elders of the Church. No, judgement fell upon them from on High because Ananias and Sapphira had enough knowledge to have walked in God's Way without telling lies, especially to God! They should have known better!

Today we are dealing with the same God who never changes. Therefore men, especially mature Christians and leaders in the Body of Christ, may experience God rebuking and chastening them directly and openly when they fall into apostasy, because they should have known better!

Notice that Paul rebuked Peter **in public** for not bringing the doctrine of Christ to the Jews: again I do not notice Paul taking Peter aside and warning him, and then getting the elders to speak to him, etc. **Peter should have known better!** Christians should guard against fostering deception in the Church by protecting leaders from judgment and attributing judgment against these leaders to a spirit of division and love-lessness!

Other Matters to be Judged

Immoral conduct of professed believers in Christ is to be judged. 1 Corinthians 5 tells a sad story and closes with the apostolic injunction,

> *'Therefore put away from among yourselves that wicked person.'* (1 Corinthians 5:13)

Disputes between Christians concerning *'things that pertain to this life'* (1 Corinthians 16:3) should be judged by a tribunal of fellow Christians instead of going before unbelievers in the civil courts. The whole sixth chapter of 1 Corinthians makes clear God's plan for His people in this regard. And some startling truths are here revealed. First, *'The saints shall judge the world.'* Second, *'We shall judge angels'* (fallen) (1 Corinthians 6:2–3). Beloved, are we letting God prepare us for this high place?

We ought to judge ourselves.

> *'Examine yourselves, whether ye be in the faith; prove your own selves.'* (2 Corinthians 13:5)

> *'For if we would judge ourselves, we should not be judged. But when we are judged, we are chastened* (child trained) *of the Lord, that we should not be condemned with the world.'*
>
> (1 Corinthians 11:31–32)

What a change and what a blessing it would be if we would judge our own faults as uncharitably as we do the faults of others, and if we would judge the failings of others as charitably as we do our own! And Christians could save themselves much chastening of the Lord if they would judge and confess and cease their disobedience to God. And, O how much dishonour and lack of fruit would our blessed Lord be spared!

Limitations of Human Judgement

Do not judge scruples. God forbids our judging our brethren concerning the eating of certain kinds of food, keeping of days, etc. Romans 14, 1 Corinthians 10:23–33 and Colossians 2:16–17 cover this subject.

Do not judge motives. See 1 Corinthians 4:1–5. Only God can see into the heart and know the motives that underlie actions.

Not as to who are saved.

> *'The Lord knoweth them that are His.'*
> (2 Timothy 2:19)

We cannot look into anyone's heart and say whether or not they have accepted the Lord Jesus Christ as their personal Saviour, if they profess that they have. But we had better test ourselves according to 2 Corinthians 5:17:

> *'If any man be in Christ, he is a new creature: old things are passed away, behold, all things are become new.'*

If this change has not taken place, our profession is vain.

Two Elements in Judgement

The New Testament Greek word that is most often translated 'judge' or 'judgement' is *'krino'*. On the one hand, it means to distinguish, to decide, to determine, to conclude, to try, to think and to call in question. That is what God wants His children to do as to whether preachers, teachers, and their teachings are true or false to His Word. The Apostle Paul writes:

> *'And this I pray, that your love may abound yet more and more in* **knowledge** *and in all* **judgement***; that ye may approve things that are excellent.'*
> (Philippians 1:9–10)

A wrong idea of love and lack of knowledge and judgement causes God's people often to approve things that are anything but excellent in God's sight. The epistle to the Hebrews tells us that mature believers, that is, those who are of 'full age', are *'those who by reason of use have their senses exercised to discern both good and evil'* (Hebrews 5:14).

On the other hand, the Greek word *'krino'* – judge or judgement – means condemn, to sentence and to punish. This is God's prerogative for He has said,

> *'Vengeance is Mine, I will repay, saith the Lord.'*
> (Romans 12:19)

Guard Against a Wrong Attitude

Christians should watch against the tendency of the flesh to assume a critical and censorious attitude toward those who do not share our opinions about other matters, other than those which have to do with

Bible doctrine and **moral conduct**. Rather than 'pick to pieces' our brethren in Christ, it is our privilege and duty to do everything we can to encourage their spiritual up-building. We ought to love and pray for one another and consider ourselves lest we be tempted.

A Final Word

If you are saved, my reader, let us not forget that,

> *'We must all appear before the Judgment Seat of Christ.'* (2 Corinthians 5:10)

It will be well with those who are studying God's Word, walking in the light of it, living for Christ and the salvation of souls. It will go ill with those who have accepted Christ but who are living for the things of this world.

If you are a mere professor of Christ, or profess nothing, my friend, may I lovingly remind you

> *'That judgment must begin at the House of God; and if it first begin at us, what shall the end be of them that obey not the gospel of God?'*
> (1 Peter 4:17)

Delay not another moment to ask God in Jesus' Name to forgive your sins. Surrender your heart and will to the loving Saviour who died for you. Make Him the Lord of your life. Happy and blessed will you be, now and forever.

Chapter 16

Control Through Disapproval

The spirit of disapproval is a very weighty and crushing spirit in both the world and the Church. I hasten to say at once that this revelation was not my own, but mentioned to me by my friend Merle while sitting in the garden one day quite recently with friends. Merle has ministered to me on more than one occasion, and I praise God for her and bless her in His precious name.

When people give you spiritual insight into an area hitherto unknown or unfamiliar to you, the best thing is to pray into it and see what the Holy Spirit reveals. While doing this, I felt the revelation was so important it must be included in this book on betrayal, which I had thought was already complete!

Merle was shown by the Lord that a judgmental attitude towards an unsaved family member, whose lifestyle she totally disapproved of, constituted betrayal, that disapproval in fact, was a type of betrayal! We have just read Dr Van Zyl's teaching about legitimate and godly judgement and should be aware, if we were not before, of its place and importance. However, the spirit of disapproval judges ourselves and others **illegitimately**.

Have you ever said that you have forgiven someone, yet retained an inner, perhaps silent, censorious attitude towards them, so that they feel attacked, threatened, criticised, or disapproved of in your presence? Yes, even when you have not uttered a word? Do you 'glance' or 'sigh' your disapproval and make them feel uncomfortable, if not openly rebuked? What about sulking?

I am sure that you have heard the expressions 'if looks could kill', 'black look', 'face like thunder'. These are expressions of disapproval which seek to threaten, intimidate and control. Again I have to point out this is witchcraft, and all witchcraft is linked to betrayal. Remember it is very hard work trying to please a demon, and the function of this spirit is to manifest disapproval. Do not try to please a demon. You must resist it, fight it.

The spirit of disapproval produces control, inertia, inactivity or ineffectual activity, even paralysis. It exhausts you, making you feel heavy, tired, boring, bored and dull. When under its influence you are made to feel slightly guilty, inadequate, suspected and under reproach, which of course you are because you have not truly been forgiven, and therefore are not free from accusation!

Let me give you an example. I spent not a few years in a lovely church where we all ministered to one another with great spontaneity and freedom. The Pastor changed, and the new one was not into our deliverance sessions. He actually disapproved of them, so that eventually we all felt terribly intimidated in his presence, tongue-tied and hesitant.

Now I am certain nobody could ever imagine me being tongue-tied, but truly I was! It took me months to realise that I was being controlled by intimidation. I was never accused of being out of order, or anything at all in fact. But if I was ministering, or even simply praying for a brother or sister in Christ, the said gentleman would take up a position reasonably close to me with arms folded and just stare at me totally expressionlessly.

I longed to be advised if I was doing anything wrong. I made such requests often, but never once was accused of anything. The silence was deafening! Of course I eventually left there and have had three glorious years of freedom to move out, led by the Holy Spirit, since that awful time. But so well I recall the infliction of a sort of inertia, paralysis, uselessness that shrouded me in that place. I use the word 'shroud' advisedly because the disapproval hung over me like a deathly pall. I felt reproached and scorned.

Those few lines from Psalm 69:20 describe absolutely how I used to feel (King James Version, then Amplified):

> 'Reproach hath broken my heart, and I am full of heaviness.'

> 'Insults and reproach have broken my heart, I am full of heaviness and distressingly sick.'

Readers may recall the heaviness, the feeling of being lifeless, mutilated, amputated, rendered incapable, unfit for battle which I described in the chapters on ME in *The Anointing Breaks the Yoke*. The last chapter of that book on betrayal has set so many people free, I give all the glory and honour to Jesus and my thanks to the sweet Holy Spirit for His incredible revelation. But I see now quite clearly that disapproval is yet another facet of treachery and again, treachery is at its most effective where there has been a relationship of trust built up, and therefore properly expected, over a period of time.

Let me give you a few more examples. Are you joyfully on the telephone to someone when the spirit of disapproval (in a person of course) enters the room or house, and you find your conversation flow stops? You feel listened to, unnatural, and your joy cuts out? Are you suddenly made to feel guilty when truly you know you haven't done anything? Beware, it's the spirit of control through disapproval.

Have you ever placed a meal on the table, a perfectly good meal, and sensed disapproval because someone at the table does not deem it their favourite food and would prefer an alternative? You may start to feel guilty, that preparing the meal has all been a waste of time, and utterly condemned. You cannot eat yours then anyway, your stomach feels heavy, tight, even sick.

Not a word of reproach is uttered but it's all in the eyes, the body language. Body language is a great conveyer of the spirit of disapproval! Controlling disapproval manifests in criticism, accusation, judgmentalism, condemnation, anger, envy, unforgiveness.

A major function of this spirit is to rob one of joy. It is a beautiful day, the sun is shining, the birds are twittering and just to be alive is so wonderful. Your senses to God's creation are so sharp, like a finely-tuned instrument. Then along comes disapproval. Results? You feel utterly blunted in your responses, the whole scene is darkened, you cannot actually hear the birds now, everything has faded, especially **joy**.

If you are a joyful person, and we should be naturally joyful because we know Jesus, the spirit of disapproval will do its utmost to rob you of that joy. There may be jealousy that you have that joy, you may be resented, even accused (silently of course) for responding to God's creation with joy. Disapproval cannot grasp or endure joy!

Jesus told the Pharisees in John 8:15:

> *'Ye judge after the flesh; I judge no man.'*

If we judge by human standards we are in real danger of God's judgement (Romans 2:1–3).

The spirit of disapproval will ultimately crush and break our spirits. A broken spirit continually leaks, is unable to hold on to healing, blessing, hope or joy. Like a cracked vessel it continually needs topping up.

There are many references by David in the Psalms to a broken spirit. God promises us in His Word that He will never do this, Isaiah 42:3:

> *'A broken reed shall he not break, a smoking flax shall he not quench: he shall bring forth judgment* (justice, right) *unto truth.'*

Isaiah 57:16 is also a beautiful reference to this promise:

> *'For I will not contend for ever, neither will I be always wroth; for the spirit should* (NKJV: would) *fail before me, and the soul which I have made.'*   (KJV)

'For I will not contend (NIV: accuse) *forever, neither will I be angry always, for (if I did stay angry) the spirit of man would faint and be consumed before Me, and (My purpose in) creating the souls of men would be frustrated.'*

(Amplified)

If you have a crushed spirit you need first to repent of the sins it has caused in you which keep the wound open, e.g: unforgiveness, anger, criticism, accusation, judging, betrayal, and **pride** which is the root of them all. If you act in any of these manners you are frankly opening yourself up to the risk of allowing the spirit of disapproval to enter.

Merle so aptly describes the spirit of disapproval as 'a heavily disguised unforgiving spirit which forgives the sin but not the sinner'. Oh, how true this is! I have seen it so many times in ministry. Recipients of prayer standing in front of you saying 'Yes, I've forgiven Alfred, Peter or Joan of adultery' and indeed they may have, but they have not forgiven the sinner.

A test is when you ask them to bless those who have despitefully used them. A look of unbelief and reluctance crosses their faces. They are feeling you are being hard, that you do not understand what Fred or Mary did to them. They might even mouth the blessing but your spirit tells you it's lip service only, and frankly the ministry cannot go on. A lot of self-pity can become locked in with disapproval and it all grows into such torment. I truly believe that most of us have been there.

I know a gentleman who has been cut out of a family will. It is really an unlawful cutting off from his inheritance and every time something crops up to indicate the family's prosperity he says, 'Well, bless them, they are welcome to it anyway' with his lips, but in his heart he's saying, 'They've got my share'!

Deep unforgiveness leaves open sores, and I tell you, brothers and sisters, there is no balm, no ointment, no cream to heal these sores.

Twenty years ago before I got born again, I worked closely with a doctor who was a dab hand at clearing up grotty skins. He himself was a basic believer and trotted out not a few pearls of wisdom. In his lectures he used to say, re. intractable skin problems, 'It's not always what gets under your skin, but who', and 'It may be not what you're eating, but what's eating you.'

To continue in unforgiveness is equal to the spirit of disapproval. It is sin, transgression, and the way of the transgressor is hard! Don't go on in such trespass because if you do you will not be a friend of the Lord Jesus, nor will you enjoy His peace and joy (Psalm 68:21).

As a clinical practitioner I see many patients, both male and female, plagued by prematurely thinning hair or even baldness. We know both can be a curse, the Scriptures say so, and I often sense that the worldly expression, 'Well, on your head be it' has a very biblical basis, as made clear in Psalm 7:16:

> *'His mischief shall return upon his own head and his violent dealing shall come down upon his own pate.'*

Pate, by the way, is the crown of the head. I really recommend anyone with such troubles to get their concordance and search the Scriptures for such revelations.

Sores anywhere which refuse to be healed will close up when there is deep repentance of unforgiveness, and then walking in that forgiveness. Involvement in the occult can also cause sores that do not respond to diet, vitamins or minerals which would normally clear the wound up in a few weeks or even days. Zinc is an incredible wound healer, and if its application or consumption does not help quite dramatically I get suspicious. Of course there are always exceptions to everything I say or write, but I do ask readers to examine their hearts for those terrible twin spirits, disapproval and unforgiveness.

My whole life's work is discerning the network of links between disease, habits, intentions, motives, resentments and so on. Satan is a crafty blinder of the eyes and in most cases when we are looking at others we also need to look hard at ourselves! As that old doctor friend of mine used to say, 'When you point a finger at someone, remember there are always three fingers pointing back at you!'

It's all very tough, but very healing, praise the Lord!

I mentioned earlier that under the influence of a spirit of disapproval you can feel guilty, inadequate, under reproach, scorned, full of heaviness, sick in the gut, sick, helpless, even lifeless.

A lot of sick people are actually nursed by relatives and loved ones who in fact have not forgiven them for being sick, because of the inconvenience it causes! Most healthy folks cannot take too much sickness, once it causes inconvenience and necessitates personal sacrifice. May the Lord bless, protect and succour all those 'nurses' who do not make their patients feel they are a problem. I marvel at the tender loving care I see in some Christian husbands for sick wives, and in Christian wives for sick husbands, and it blesses and blesses me to witness such unconditional love, believe me.

Of course there are many other kinds of demands, inconvenience or disappointment which can bring annoyance, unforgiveness and disapproval within family, church or workplace. Below is a check list for when this spirit is operating against you.

1. You feel guarded in speech and action in its presence, and worry afterwards in case you said or did something wrong.
2. Even innocent comments make you feel got at.
3. You react defensively to justify yourself.
4. A particular look can cause your joyful mood to change to one of anxiety or uncertainty.
5. You need to check a person's reaction before making a decision, to ensure their approval.
6. You need reassurance of their love, affection or approval.

Make a list of all those you feel may genuinely disapprove of you. Do not allow high imagination to run away with you. List only those where there is real witness of disapproval. Call this List 1.

Disapproval judges all the time. It compares another's behaviour with how it would behave, and then finds them lacking or wanting. It is rooted in pride: understand that humility and disapproval cannot be partners! Please read Matthew 7:1–5 again:

> 'Judge not, that ye be not judged. For with what judgment ye judge, ye shall be judged; and with

*what measure ye mete, it shall be measured to you
again. And why beholdest thou the mote that is in
thy brother's eye, but considerest not the beam
that is in thine own eye? Or how wilt thou say to
thy brother, Let me pull out the mote out of thine
eye; and, behold, a beam is in thine own eye? Thou
hypocrite, first cast out the beam out of thine own
eye; and then shalt thou see clearly to cast out the
mote out of thy brother's eye.'*

Please be careful to understand the following: when
you judge illegitimately you take on a role which only
God has, that of being The Judge. Not only have you
usurped a place and authority which is not yours, but
you have presumed to do God's job for Him. **While
you are in that place, God will not move or act on
behalf of you, the defendant**.

Merle gave the picture of a court case, in which
God the Father is like the Judge and Jesus is our
lawyer. Jesus can present and plead our case before
the Judge far more knowingly and favourably than
we can on our own behalf. However, if we do not
completely release our plea or complaint into Jesus'
hands, we interfere with His management of the case.
The Judge cannot then reach a decision, and we do
not receive the abundant settlement Jesus has already
won for us! So, we are actually standing between
**God our vindication, and help for the other person as
well**.

> *'Beloved, never avenge yourselves but **leave the
> way open** for God's wrath.'*
>
> (Romans 12:19, Amplified)

164

Not only does a judgmental form of control bind the person operating in it, but it prevents the very one they disapprove of from getting free. It binds them together: *'Judge not that ye be not judged!'*

Make a list of those you disapprove of. Check off how many names are the same as those on List 1. See how this spiritual principle of the judged becoming the judging, and vice-versa, works out?

So disapproval is unforgiveness. It disapproves of the person while professing to forgive their behaviour. 1 Corinthians 13:5b says love *'keeps no record of wrongs'*. Disapproval is the enemy of love and unity. **It may be envious, and try to pull down the person it feels envious of**.

Often the origin of this spirit comes from being brought up to believe love is conditional, performance-linked. You are loved until you make a mistake, then you forfeit that love. It becomes impossible to believe love doesn't equal approval. You carry this on by witholding your approval when you are displeased.

Significantly this also affects how you view your salvation because its message is a **direct contradiction to the message of the cross**. You may find it impossible to come fully into your own free, unearned acceptance and forgiveness by Christ, until that stronghold of disapproval has been broken and your healing can begin. Another root is when disapproval becomes your defence against feeling disapproved of (and all the hurt that comes with that, including strong feelings of treachery and betrayal).

Some Questions

Is it possible you might be moving in disapproval? Is your prayer life successful or disappointing? Check out pride and judging (in which God resists you), unforgiveness (God will not hear you) and disunity (no blessing).

Apart from obvious times of verbal disagreement, criticism, correction, or even getting cross, how do you register your disapproval? A black look? Tight lips? Silence? Sulking? All these are common signals of disapproval, and note: they are mainly **non-verbal**.

Why don't we voice our hidden disapproval more? Is it because we're unsure of our right to make a judgment? Is it because we know it is actually none of our business? Do we find it fairly easy to speak out our disapproval only in circumstances where we feel that reaction is legitimate, e.g. parent/child, teacher/pupil, etc.?

Is it easier to be real in our reactions when we know our heart is right towards the person, even when we find what they are doing unacceptable? It should be possible for us to love and forgive the sinner while protesting about the sin, whereas the spirit of disapproval does the opposite!

What to Do

How do we handle unrighteous and ungodly behaviour? **In the Spirit.**

> 'Brethren, if any person is overtaken in misconduct or sin of any sort, you who are spiritual (who are responsive to and controlled by the Spirit) should set him right and restore and reinstate him, **without any sense of superiority and with all gentleness**, keeping an attentive eye on yourself lest you should be tempted also.'
>
> (Galatians 6:1, Amplified)

166

This confirms John 8:15, when Jesus said that He only judged by the Spirit.

We love the sinner but hate the sin. We guard our hearts from the sins of wrong reactions, pride, judgment, criticism, bitterness, unforgiveness and we **love** and **pray** for them. We prepare ourselves to **speak, confront, challenge if (but only if!)** the Holy Spirit tells us to.

Control binds. It is a two-way bondage. You need to free, and to be set free, from that control. Only when this sin has been dealt with can the wounds begin to heal. Read Isaiah 57:18–19 for God's promise:

> '*I have seen his ways, and will heal him: I will lead him also, and restore comfort unto him and to his mourners. I create the fruit of his lips: Peace, peace to him that is far off, and to him that is near, saith the Lord; and I will heal him.*'

We also:
1. Repent of judging and criticising,
2. Repent of controlling by disapproval, and
3. Forgive and release into acceptance.
4. Repent of allowing ourselves to be controlled by disapproval.
5. Repent of self-disapproval.
6. Break the power of the spirit of disapproval, and separate our soul and spirit to God, away from those disapproving of us, and then from those we have disapproved of.
7. Ask the Holy Spirit to start the healing process.
8. Start to move out in the opposite spirit, i.e: **acceptance**. See all of Matthew 5 for the

principles operating in this action. It is very important. It is the action we must put together with our faith. (It is also very costly and a worthy sacrifice.)

I realise that some of what I received on treachery and betrayal by revelation and recorded earlier in this book is actually interwoven with Merle's revelation. I described how she received and gave this to me when I was on the verge of finishing the manuscript with the previous chapter, or so I thought! That is how our Father works!

I have often found it quite staggering that people in very different circumstances who spend time in the closet hear God saying much the same thing. Our various personal situations give it a slightly different slant or colour, whilst it is all part of the same fabric.

It's rather like a brightly woven carpet, full of vague designs but, for example, in each corner one can clearly pick out a rose or a leaf. Having done that, one can then discern that the remainder forms into some sort of garden, but one had to see the rose clearly before the rest of the pattern, and what it represented, could become evident. I hope I am making myself clear.

Merle really gave me a gold nugget in sharing this personal experience of how the Lord convicted her that forgiving what others **had done**, while not forgiving **them**, is sin. We didn't have long enough to delve deeply into it on that sunny afternoon in my garden when we were also sharing with two others, but I chewed on what she said for a very considerable time.

I asked her to send me her study notes on what the Lord had shown her about disapproval and they arrived on my desk as I reached the last chapter. I get such a copious mail to open, and those items which will take deep personal discernment get popped back into their envelopes and put by my bedside or on the pending tray of my desk.

I cannot tell you how many constant interruptions, quite demonic, there were to prevent me studying the contents of her package before this manuscript, which has all been written very quickly in a few weeks, was popped off to the publisher! I think the devil was intent on my not getting this further spiritual insight into print, but our prayers for the manuscript prevailed, and I pray that you will experience the awesomeness and the depth of this revelation and ask the Holy Spirit to convict you if it is an area you need to deal with.

I am constantly astonished at how many different facets there are of deliverance ministry. Whilst having to look at the intricate, I continually return and cling to the simplicity of the truth concerning the fear of the Lord. I found myself quite comforted, after reading all this on disapproval, to go back over the scriptures in Chapter 21 of *The Anointing Breaks the Yoke*, entitled 'The Fear of the Lord'.

Again I was reminded that an awesome fear of the Lord is one of the greatest safeguards against control. Fear of man manipulates. It is a spirit which backs disapproval. The fear of the Lord is the beginning of wisdom, and frankly we cannot get enough of it.

If only we, all of us, could realise just how awesome is our living God we would be well on the way to shedding the shackles of control emanating from the fear of man, and be fearfully aware of the punishment for controlling others, in whatever way. It is a time for plain unvarnished honesty, folks, and remember how subtle the enemy is. It is only the truth that sets us free, as it is written.

Bless you for hanging in there, the Lord be praised!

Chapter 17

The Treachery of Freemasonry

Louise arrived at the Clinic on 20th September 1994. I had answered her telephone enquiry about the Clinic myself, and felt a tremendous anointing as we spoke. I knew immediately that ultimately I should minister to her.

Louise had an impediment in her speech which provoked a need for much patience. As she poured out her woes I received the words 'Masonic curse'. Later in the conversation it was revealed that she had not been born with it, but the impediment came when her father was promoted to the chair of his Masonic lodge and became a Worshipful Grand-Master.

Louise was a nurse and I could imagine the difficulty this impediment made in a nurse/patient relationship. I say this with love. It can be quite exhausting even for well people to have to wait for a person's conversation punctuated with a stammer. But I will let this precious twenty-eight year old tell her own story.

Louise's Testimony

'I was born a perfectly healthy child, full of energy and vitality, physically fit and well. Suddenly at six years old I developed a pronounced speech impediment, which the medical profession related to being a result of stress and nervousness. During this time my father had joined Freemasonry with the encouragement of my grandfather, who was a dominant character over our lives. Coming from Scottish origins, Freemasonry goes back through several generations in my family tree.

My brother, mother and myself all became Christians as the result of a local seaside beach mission, and so there was always conflict between good and evil throughout my family life. As I entered into my early twenties I started to develop several strange viral infections which would leave me feeling extremely debilitated.

I met the man whom I was to marry at the age of twenty-one. He became a Christian soon after we became engaged. Unfortunately my marriage ended rather traumatically and suddenly, after only sixteen months of us being together. During that time I became chronically unwell with glandular fever and Post-Viral Fatigue Syndrome. My husband committed acts which were against his Christian beliefs, including mental abuse, bullying, dishonesty and adultery. The lying and deceit finally drove us apart.

My parents were supportive and understanding but suddenly became over-protective towards me. I felt under manipulation, domination and control and too weak to make decisions for myself, mostly through fear of making another mistake. I took on sole responsibility of the matrimonial home, and gave my ex-husband the freedom of starting a new life once again as a single man. I really wanted to leave the house but it would not sell.

The next three years were a constant struggle to heal a broken heart, cope with the persistent Post-Viral Fatigue Syndrome and endure the pain and discomfort of Irritable Bowel Syndrome. I suffered with continuous oral and vaginal infections, mood swings, hormone imbalances, and food cravings and would binge excessively on a high sugar and carbohydrate diet.

My over-eating resulted in nausea, constipation, exhaustion and frequent sick leave from work. My trips to my doctor increased. He took blood tests but could not discover the reason for my ill health. I constantly worried about the finances, my job, current studies and maintaining my home with all its bad memories of past years.

Just when I was at my lowest ebb I met my new fiancé, through the local Baptist church, and as he too had suffered similar circumstances we soon became firm friends. I explained to him how I felt that the Lord had spoken to me through His Word, Deuteronomy 4, that there was a curse over my family which needed to be broken. My father had just finished his nine months of being the Worshipful Grand Master in Freemasonry.

My fiancé, having received some deliverance himself, introduced me to a lovely Christian couple who were full-time deliverance ministers. I experienced some release with a variety of manifestations from within me, and there was some improvement in my health generally. I renounced all past occult experience in my life such as acupuncture, karate, homoeopathy and self-hypnotherapy. My spiritual walk with the Lord was now much closer. However, my digestive problems still persisted, and then a close friend of my fiancé introduced me to some literature about Pearl Coleman and her Clinic.

Pearl confirmed my illnesses and past life experiences as being related to my father's connection with Freemasonry and told me that these cords still needed to be broken. As a result of my Candida infections I had developed severe allergies to a variety of foods, including having a sodium toxicity. I was placed on a food programme and prescribed a course of vitamin and mineral supplements to strengthen my immune system. During this time I was struggling with finances and desperately trying to sell my home. We were planning to get engaged and my parents were not particularly delighted about the prospect, but very concerned for my welfare.

Pearl and her team prayed over me and I experienced the final release of spiritual bondage and further deliverance. The tightening in my neck disappeared, my speech flowed freely without hesitancy, and the cords released their final grip around my hands and feet.

Five weeks later the improvement is remarkable. All my food allergies have disappeared, there is an enormous improvement in my speech, and my house is in the process of being sold! My parents no longer feel the necessity to make decisions for me and they have given their blessing for us to get married. Other physical healing has been apparent. My hair has stopped falling out and now looks healthy and shiny, and my energy is slowly returning.

I have so much to thank the Lord for: complete healing both physically and mentally, a wonderful Christian man who loves me greatly, and the love and Christian ministry I have received from Pearl Coleman and her helpers. My brother and his wife have recommitted their lives to Christ and are now only too aware of the dangers of Freemasonry, having sought support and guidance from our minister. For the first time in my life I feel in control and free to make my own decisions. The person I now turn to is Jesus Christ, my loving Saviour.

> *"Repent then, and turn to God so that your sins may be wiped out, that times of refreshing may come from the Lord, and that he may send the Christ, who has been appointed for you, even Jesus."'* (Acts 3:19)

When Louise sat in front of me she told me the Freemasonry had been dealt with and I told her it had not, otherwise I would not be discerning it. She had had a great deal of ministry in sessions, but I explained that the word of God is **quick** and powerful

(Hebrews 4:12), that I'm not too much into sessions, and the longer I am in the ministry the quicker it is. I say this with no disrespect to any valiant ministry, but the Lord has clearly shown me not to make a meal of it. I say that in love.

I was prompted by the Holy Spirit to minister to Louise at once, and to anoint her tongue, throat, arms and hands, and decommission witchcraft at the feet. I broke the curse of treachery and called out the spirit which executed the curse. I decommissioned the angel of death, cut her off from Jezebel, and annulled every ungodly covenant set up against her.

The unholy trinity (Death and Hades, the Antichrist, and Jezebel) were commanded out in Jesus' name. I cut her off from her mother, both soul ties and umbilical tie were dealt with. I loved her fiancé, and prophesied over them together, and received total peace concerning his suitability as a Christian husband.

Freemasonry is of course apalling betrayal by the head of the family, when he should be safeguarding and protecting them. 'Head' in Hebrew means 'source of'. By making terrible oaths like 'may my tongue be cut out' and 'my heart be torn out', etc., etc., 'if I betray the secrets of the little black book or the lodge,' this husband and father is speaking curses over himself which flow to his family, for he is the source of their blessing or cursing. Whole families come under these terrible self-spoken curses with horrific effects. The iniquity (wickedness) of the fathers falls upon the children to the third and fourth generations, Exodus 34:7, Numbers 14:18, etc.

When this precious sister in Christ returned a month later she was radiant, free and in total charge of her life. Her house was sold, her fiancé accepted by her family. No longer was Jezebel at work in her life, the tyranny of her father had ceased. Following this wonderful news, another two patients came that same day with joyful reports of complete freedom and renewal from severe and long-term bondage from other sources. All glory, honour and praise to our mighty Lord Jesus!

Chapter 18

God Resists the Proud

I want to say a word here about those who continually cry out to God for this, that and the other, some genuine, real heart cries which appear to produce one conviction only and that is that God is deaf! Please look at Isaiah 59:1–2:

> 'Behold, the Lord's hand is not shortened, that it cannot save; neither his ear heavy, that it cannot hear: But your iniquities have separated between you and your God, and your sins have hid his face from you, that he will not hear.'

It is the **but** I should like to emphasise here. Idolatry is iniquity, and pride, so closely linked with it throughout Scripture, brings a state which renders our Father deaf. The Holy Bible says quite clearly God resists the proud:

> 'Wherefore he saith, God resisteth the proud, but giveth grace unto the humble.'   (James 4:6b)

'Likewise, ye younger, submit yourselves unto the elder. Yea, all of you be subject one to another, and be clothed with humility: for God resisteth the proud, and giveth grace to the humble. Humble yourselves therefore under the mighty hand of God that he may exalt you in due time.'

(1 Peter 5:5–6)

'Though the Lord be high, yet hath he respect unto the lowly; but the proud he knoweth afar off.'

(Psalm 138:6)

You get out your concordance and do a study on pride and humility and you'll see what I am attempting to convey to you. So many scriptures say that He exalts the humble and meek. The best-known ones are:

'Blessed are the meek: for they shall inherit the earth.'   (Matthew 5:5)

and

'Whosoever exalteth himself shall be abased; and he that humbleth himself shall be exalted.'

(Luke 14:11 – important enough to be repeated in Luke 18:14)

But there are also less well-known scriptures which emphasise this:

'The Lord lifteth up the meek: he casteth the wicked down to the ground.'   (Psalm 147:6)

> *'Pride goeth before destruction, and an haughty spirit before a fall.'*   (Proverbs 16:18)

> *'By humility and the fear of the Lord are riches, and honour, and life.'*   (Proverbs 22:4)

> *'For thus saith the high and lofty One that inhabiteth eternity, whose name is Holy; I dwell in the high and holy place, with him also that is of a contrite and humble spirit, to revive the spirit of the humble, and to revive the heart of the contrite ones.'*   (Isaiah 57:15)

> *'Let the brother of low degree rejoice in that he is exalted: but the rich, in that he is made low: because as the flower of the grass he shall pass away.'*   (James 1:9–10)

Rich does not necessarily mean in terms of finances either, but spiritually blessed.

I recently had quite a few scriptures for someone, which I had tended to store up because of their lack of receptivity. I had brought scriptures in love to that person before and they had been received with scepticism, almost as if I had made up that I had heard from the Lord. However, I am definitely not a 'thus saith' because I tremble in awe at the word of God, I really do. I also tremble for those who scoff at it and treat what one brings in love with contempt. The scriptures are clear that we should tremble at the word of God:

> *'But to this man will I look, even to him that is poor and of a contrite spirit, and trembleth at my word.'*   (Isaiah 66:2b–c)

> *'Hear the word of the Lord, ye that tremble at his word.'* (Isaiah 66:5a)

> *'I will delight myself in thy statutes: I will not forget thy word.'* (Psalm 119:16)

Again, humility and obedience are linked together and oppose pride and idolatry. Spiritual maturity cannot come without total dependence on God. The Bible tells us even Jesus said:

> *'The Son can do nothing of himself, but what he seeth the Father do ... I can of mine own self do nothing: as I hear, I judge: and my judgment is just; because I seek not mine own will, but the will of the Father which hath sent me.'*
> (John 5:19b and 30a)

and

> *'He that abideth in me, and I in him, the same bringeth forth much fruit; for without me you can do nothing.'* (John 15:5b)

Yet all over the world, and I would say Britain and the USA in particular, there is a lot of idolatry of big ministries going on which leads to idolatry of men and empire-building for individuals in ministries, where Ishmael (the work of the flesh) is clearly produced with soul power often in its wake. Empire building can herald deception and the apostate church.

'Judgment begins at the house of God' (1 Peter 4:17) and the Church needs to get on its face and cry out

'Lord, we do not know what to do, please help us.' We need to entreat God. God has to be central. Alas, frequently He is a side-issue, an 'also-ran'.

Disillusionment in churches brings pressure to birth an Ishmael (a work of the flesh) in those churches, just to get things going, and before we know where we are, people are paying attention to the counterfeit as though it's the real thing! It's quite horrendous, it really is. Pride wants power and leadership. Please do a study of Matthew 23 which also highlights what I am saying. Jesus only ever radiated the **Father's** glory. Humility seeks servanthood in weakness. There is no godly strength except in our weakness:

> 'We preach Christ crucified ... Because the foolishness of God is wiser than men; and the weakness of God is stronger than men.'
>
> (1 Corinthians 1:23–5)

> 'My grace is sufficient for thee: for my strength is made perfect in weakness. Most gladly therefore will I rather glory in my infirmities, that the power of Christ may rest upon me. Therefore I take pleasure in infirmities, in reproaches, in necessities, in persecutions, in distresses for Christ's sake: for when I am weak, then am I strong.' (2 Corinthians 12:9b–10)

> 'The resurrection of the dead ... is sown in dishonour; it is raised in glory: it is sown in weakness; it is raised in power.' (1 Corinthians 15:42a–43b)

Scripture emphasises without doubt where our instruction is to come from. Yes, we do sit at the feet of wiser men, that is scriptural, but ultimately we need to check everything out with the word of God for ourselves, and there is no substitute for doing that. We cannot afford to be lazy and hope somebody else will tell us!

There is also a lot of dying to self to do, folks. We have to die daily.

> *'As it is written* (in Psalm 44:22)*, For thy sake we are killed all the day long; we are accounted as sheep for the slaughter.'* (Romans 8:36)

I came across a beautiful piece of writing in a Malaysian ministry booklet. It states that the author is unknown, so I cannot ask his or her permission to reprint it, and judging from the content the writer would not want publicity.

So I end this, my shortest book, on this holy note, quoting this jewel of a text and blessing that unknown author for blessing me. I trust it will bless you also, dear Reader, and that you will check up for yourselves all I bring to you in my love for the Church.

Others May, You Cannot!

If God has called you to be really like Jesus, He will draw you into a life of crucifixion and humility, and put upon you such demands of obedience that you will not be able to follow other people, or measure yourself by other Christians, and in many ways He will seem to let other people do things which He will not let you do.

Other Christians and ministers who seem very religious and useful may push themselves, pull wires and work schemes to carry out their plans, but you cannot do it, and if you attempt it you will meet with such failure and rebuke from the Lord as to make you sorely penitent.

Others may boast of themselves, of their work, of their successes, of their writings, but the Holy Spirit will not allow you to do any such thing, and if you begin it He will lead you into some deep mortification that will make you despise yourself and all your good works.

The Lord may let others be honoured and put forward, and keep you hidden in obscurity, because He wants to produce some choice, fragrant fruit for His coming glory which can only be produced in the shade. He may let others be great, and keep you small. He may let others do a work for Him and get the credit for it, but He will make you work and toil on without knowing how much you are doing; and then to make your work still more precious, He may let others get credit for the work which you have done, and thus make your reward ten times greater when Jesus comes.

The Holy Spirit will put a strict watch over you, with a jealous love, and will rebuke you for little words and feelings, or for wasting your time, which other Christians never feel distressed over. So make up your mind that God is an infinite Sovereign, and has a right to do as He pleases with His own. He may not explain to you a thousand things which puzzle your reason in His dealings with you, but if you absolutely sell yourself to be His love slave, He will wrap you up in a jealous love, and bestow upon you many blessings which come only to those who are in the inner circle.

Settle it forever then, that you are to deal directly

with the Holy Spirit, and that He must have the right to tie your tongue, or chain your hand, or close your eyes, in ways that He does not seem to use with others. Now, when you are so possessed with the living God that you are, in your secret heart, pleased and delighted over this peculiar, personal, private, jealous guardianship and management of the Holy Spirit over your life, you will have found the vestibule of Heaven.

Finale

In the midst of finalising this book the Lord required me to lay down all diagnostic tools at the Clinic, although I may be allowed to take blood pressure or pulse rate! This has cancelled out a good two-thirds of our work as there will now be no allergy-testing! We will be led by the Spirit concerning allergies, as in all things.

The Lord has shown me that this is to be an end-time Clinic, where His Church is taught not to defile the temple of the Holy Spirit (our bodies), and how the immune system can be supported with wisdom concerning food intake. This will give strength and remove dependence on drugs and medicines, as will be necessary in end times.

People who go through our regime invariably lose a stone of excess weight in one month, become extremely energetic and have excellent skin texture, as well as improvement in sight, hair and fingernails. Noticeably, when patients are working amid those with infections like influenza they do not succumb. A common report is that they 'do not catch things anymore' or if they do, they shake it off in a day.

A supplement in *The European* not long ago extolled the virtues of hydrotherapy, how rejuvenating it is, how it strengthens the immune system and makes one ageless in terms of general health. We have been insisting patients do this for 25 years, simply cold-showering for four minutes daily after a warm shower or bath. All the schedules, special requirements and instructions in the articles made very complicated what it is so simple and, properly explained, can be a part of anyone's normal morning toilet routine.

Additionally, we teach lymph brushing which is a preventative of certain cancers, including lymph and breast malignancies. We educate people not to cook with aluminium foil, utensils or cookware, nor to use aluminium deodorants. The action of aluminium in deodorants blocks the sweat glands which should eliminate toxins, amongst other functions.

Similarly, we teach patients to avoid fluoride in drops or toothpastes like the plague, because fluoride is a toxic waste by-product of the aluminium industry. It is a potent broad spectrum enzyme inhibitor, interfering with the reproduction system, kidneys, mucous membrane, skin, joints and neuro-muscular system, etc. All this is well documented in medical literature, and references can be supplied to those interested.

There is tremendous betrayal not only of the Church but of the public in general where chemicals are produced as toxic waste by-products, not to mention those purpose-made for fertilisers, foods, medicines, etc., and where the over-riding aim of maximising income and profits results in damage to health and welfare. But we too can betray ourselves by supporting or assisting in this damage.

I cannot stress enough that people would not put into their cars the sort of rubbish they put into their bodies, and still expect a good performance. Cars are usually treated nicely, bodies are invariably abused and submitted to a daily technological 'feast' which does far more harm than good. It is only by the mercy of God and the wonderful compensating mechanisms He has put into the body that we do not feel such effects far more, but eventually even those are overcome! Many Christians are simply doing a good cover-up job with prayer, when they should be laying the axe to the root of the tree.

So important do I feel it is to get this information over to the Church, which is desperately ignorant in these areas (Hosea 4:6), that I am praying about commencing day-long seminars on 'Divine Health', to teach people wisdom on hygiene, diet and general health habits in order to enable them to run the race with strength, instead of depleted immune systems and seemingly endless infirmities. This would enable those who cannot afford private two-hour initial consultations to come and reap the benefits of my wider experience of some 40 years in these areas, for only approximately £50 for a full day, depending on venue and numbers. If you feel there would be an interest in this in the Body, please let us know (and enclose a stamped, self-addressed envelope for a reply).

I am training assistants to do this work to keep the Clinic running apart from the ministry. Yet they cannot always be purely voluntary workers, because of their own costs and domestic overheads. This is not a new problem. One of Paul's helpers nearly died trying to make up for the general lack of support even to him from the Body of Christ!

> *'Epaphroditus, my brother, and companion in labour, and fellowsoldier, but your messenger, and he that ministered to my wants ... was sick nigh unto death; but God had mercy on him; and not on him only, but on me also, lest I should have sorrow upon sorrow ... because for the work of Christ he was nigh unto death, not regarding his life, to supply your lack of service to me.'*
>
> (Philippians 2:25–30)

So I include a prayer that you will at least be inspired to purchase not only mine, but frutiful Christian books and tapes, etc. generally, and not borrow or pass them on to another 10 people! This might sound a bit tough or out of order, but the Church does not seem aware that Christian book shops are in serious difficulties and many have closed because of the recession in book sales and the numerous accounts never paid up!

Donations also seem to have acquired a bad reputation from a few large 'media' ministries where they have been abused. But if you do not sow into those suppliers and ministries which really bless and help you, when you – and others dear to you – really need them you may be surprised to find they have gone!

Many have grown up completely outside the church or state systems and have no other means of income than purchases or contributions from those blessed by their work. Buying books or tapes, and recommending others to do so, provides a small contribution towards their many running and overhead costs incurred in service to the Body of Christ.

New Wine Press, which has published all my books, is also a wonderful ministry and mission in itself, especially to India and Africa. The books are available from us or Christian Bookshops, and should be read in the following order to understand clearly what and how God has taught me:

1. *Go and Do Likewise* £3.50
2. *Fruit Abiding in the Vine* £3.50
3. *The Anointing Breaks the Yoke* (with revelation on ME and the Angel of Death) £4.50
4. *Jehovah Jireh (The Lord My Provider)* £4.99
5. *On the Night He was Betrayed (Treachery and Betrayal in the Church)*, also with revelation on breaking Asian strongholds.
6. Coming shortly: *Refined by Fire.*

Our address is: **Christian Clinic for Environmental Medicine**, 'Lane End', Highlands Lane, Westfield, Woking, Surrey GU22 9PU. Please make cheques payable to **Pearl A. Coleman** and include estimated postage and packing allowing for postal charge increases as they occur.

Thank you for your loving support. Please remember to pray for the Jews, the Clinic and City of God Ministries as well as our faithful team and intercessors.

If you need to get yourself in order physically, mentally or spiritually, please send a large A4 SAE with 36p postage (adjusted if rates increase) for Clinic information, but without a ten-page letter enclosed. If we are to minister to you we do not need the gory details, only the Holy Spirit!

May God bless you richly for reading this book. Know that I love you.

In His holy name, your servant,

Pearl Coleman Kumar

Further Information

Please Note
If any church, fellowship, or group would like me to
bring this message to their assembly, I will be
delighted to serve you in this way.

Pearl Coleman Kumar

Christian Clinic for Environmental Medicine
(or: CCEM)

> 'Lane End', Highlands Lane
> Westfield, Woking
> Surrey GU22 9PU.

(Please make any cheques payable to P.A. Coleman,
and to include estimated postage and packing if
possible. Thank you.)

For those who have not been notified, the address for
Barry Smith's books, which detail how the end time
one world system is being set up right under our
noses, but hidden from our eyes, is now changed to:

Penfold Book and Bible House International
(or: PBBHI)

> PO Box 26
> Bicester
> Oxfordshire OX6 8PB